Over Time

Coach Katte on Basketball and Life

Coach Dick Katte & Mark Wolf

Blue River Press
Indianapolis

www.brpressbooks.com

Over Time: Coach Katte on Basketball and Life © 2014 Dick Katte
ISBN: 9781935628422
Library of Congress Control Number: 2014948374

Cover designed by Phil Velikan
Cover photo by Cory Brangoccio
Packaged by Wish Publishing

Printed in the United States of America
10 9 8 7 6 5 4 3 2

Published by Blue River Press
Indianapolis, Indiana
(800) 296-0481
A Tom Doherty Company, Inc., Imprint

Distributed in the United States by
Cardinal Publishers Group
www.cardinalpub.com

I dedicate this book to my wife, Lorraine, who has always been the love of my life and a very Christ-like companion. Without her, I would not be what I am today. She became my best assistant coach and my faithful scribe. She has also been very understanding while I have been immersed in this project. "Many women do noble things, but you surpass them all." Proverbs 31:29 — Dick Katte

For Cheryl, the inspiration for everything good that happens in my life. And to Matthew, Michael, Lisa, Kate, Anabelle and Leila, for making that life so rewarding. — Mark Wolf

Coach Dick Katte swept the floor before every practice so that his players would have a good playing surface. (Photo by Andy Cross, The Denver Post)

Acknowledgements

As I reflect on the people and events that contributed to my life and my basketball career, I wish to first of all acknowledge my wife. Lorraine has been by my side throughout my adult life, has been to more basketball games than I can count, and has been my support through adversities and celebrations. Together, we can testify to the faithfulness of God through the experiences we have shared in coaching, caring and loving.

And to my children, I acknowledge that at times I spent more time with other people's children than with my own, and yet the joys and special moments we shared are very memorable to me. With son, Keith, I cherish the moments we spent together at home, and at school, in basketball, and in coaching. I always valued his perspective—the many moments we stood together through life and basketball.

With our daughter, Jamie, the ups and downs of her battle with leukemia over the past several years has taught me how insignificant the win-loss syndrome of basketball really is… It was good to be with her in Seattle on several occasions while she was in treatment at the Fred Hutchinson Cancer Center and the Seattle Cancer Care Alliance as we tried to walk beside her and support her in her fight against leukemia. While we sat together, she edited some of the chapters in this book. It was touching as we shared some of my life story and her memories of it. She lost her battle for life as this book was at the publisher. She was so proud that once again she was in remission, but died due to complications following her second stem cell transplant. She touched many lives with her beautiful smile, positive attitude, courage, determination and perseverance.

To Shelly and Laurie, I acknowledge their gifts as daughters, wives, mothers, and teachers. Much of the love and care of your mother is evident in you and your families. Both daughters found time to be my statisticians in games so they could be a part of my life. Our journey together included attending many events and celebrations and enjoying their children and our grandchildren.

Throughout the years, I have been blessed to have assistant coaches who were committed to young people and loved basketball. I placed a high value on their input in practice, planning, game decisions, and in relationships with players. They have been very loyal and supportive to the program at Denver Christian and to me as the head basketball coach.

As I list them alphabetically I thank them sincerely: Mark Bender, Jim Boonstra, Stan Cole, Jim De Groot, Gene De Haan, Bill Dekkinga, Ben Dirkson, Andy Draayer, Eldon Dyk, Brett Hatch, Steve Heerema, Cliff Hendrick, Tim Hoeksema, Brad Homan, Keith Katte, Ben Kurtz, Jeff Mains, Rich Schemper, Russ Smith, Dave Tanis, Mark Swalley, Tyler Van Eps, Ray Van Heukelem (32 years), Jim Warren, Jim Woudstra, and Tom Young.

Besides family and coaches there are other who I acknowledge because of their impact on my career. My colleagues at Denver Christian High School showed strong support for my teaching and coaching. Al TeBrink and Dr. De Roos dependably and expertly ran the scoreboards for all of my 52 years at Denver Christian and were very supportive fans. Curt Youngsma faithfully kept my scorebook for many years at our home games and Brad Lanser followed him. Many other faithful supporters made my job as athletic director easier by always volunteering at Denver Christian during home games. Friend Al Cok stood by my side as advisor as well as advocate; I cherished his insights on basketball and life.

My 40 year relationship with the Colorado High School Activities Association cultivated a great appreciation for integrity, loyalty, and commitment of people dedicated to high school students: people like Paul Angelico, Bert Borgmann, Bob Cates, Rhonda Blanford-Green, Chuck Howell, Bob Ottewill, Bill Reader, Tom Robinson, and many others are just quality!

My association and jobs in the Metropolitan League were also a 40-year journey with many good memories and lasting friendships with Skip Bennett, Chris Bullard, Ed Caruso, Mike Gabriel, Warren Kettner, Terry Miller, Loren Otte, Todd Schayes, Al Villani, Art Wollenweber, and others. They were strong leaders for the league for many years.

Another family of colleagues and friends is a result of my 16-year career as a football official in the Western Athletic Conference. My supervisor, John Adams, was a recognized leader with great expertise in football rules, and I am grateful for his confidence in me.

When I look back at 52 years in coaching and teaching I must say I was blessed beyond measure. This book is my way of giving back because I was so richly given to. My prayer would be that when people read this book they can be reminded how great it is to work with young people and to make a difference in their lives.

— Dick Katte

This book could not have been written without Lorraine and Dick Katte allowing me to share their lives during countless hours at their kitchen table and elsewhere. My wife, Cheryl, was supportive through every step of the process. Her keen reader's eye improved the manuscript immeasurably.

My parents, Katie and the late Charlie Wolf, have given me love and support throughout my life as well as a rich appreciation for a life of public service. I had good teachers at North White High School, especially Karen Luke, a fine editor and journalism teacher who encouraged a small town kid to pursue a career in journalism, and Miss Bertha Bostick, whose exacting standards for English composition taught me that craft is in the details.

I am fortunate to have been able to learn from talented co-workers from the Arvada Citizen-Sentinel to the Charlotte Observer, the Rocky Mountain News and now at the National Conference of State Legislatures. The evocative photo of Dick that appears on the cover of this book was taken by Cory Brangoccio, a talented young photographer whose mother, Kathy works in the office next to mine at NCSL. As fate would have it, Kathy and I did not meet until after Cory's photo became our leading choice for the cover.

The exceptional high school sports coverage throughout Dick's career by the Rocky Mountain News (especially Scott Stocker and Gerry Valerio) and The Denver Post (Neil Devlin and his crew) provided a rich source of research and allowed us to jog our memories about long-ago games.

Thanks to all the coaches who have allowed me to coach with and for them in the Columbine basketball program: Rudy Martin, Clay Thielking, Brandon Brookfield, Jeff Wennberg, Ed Corridori, Neil Patterson, John Suder, David Berghoefer, Brian Hunt and both Lorens Knudsens. And to Frank DeAngelis, the Columbine principal whose resilience, strength and enthusiasm has inspired thousands of students.

— Mark Wolf

We would like to jointly acknowledge the support from Tom Doherty at Blue River Press and Cardinal Publishers Group for making this book possible.

Table of Contents

Foreword

My first encounter with Dick Katte was in the late '70s when I was starting out as a high school basketball official. I was nervous to be going into the Quonset hut that passed for a gym at Denver Christian and to be working for a coach who had already planted the seeds of a legendary career. I shouldn't have worried. The kids, the fans, the gym and especially the coach were first class, what you'd idealize as the perfect atmosphere for a high school basketball game.

I got to know Dick better when he became my "boss" as a member of the Colorado High School Activities Association Executive Committee. I had just taken over as Commissioner in 1990 and was facing a number of serious challenges, particularly related to finances. As if setting up a game plan against a big rival or solving a mathematical equation, Dick was a pragmatist, a voice of reason that never lingered in the past but always looked forward to solutions. He had a real impact in turning around CHSAA, in setting it on solid ground so it could face the increasing demands placed on it by the growing emphasis (or overemphasis) of high school athletic competition.

From there, I got to know Dick and his wife Lorraine as friends. They were always delightful to spend time with — both serious professionals who knew how to have fun after a day's work. They loved people and loved life — and especially each other.

To have a book containing Dick Katte's thoughts about basketball and life is a true gift. We have Mark Wolf to thank for approaching Dick in the final week of his last season of coaching (2011-2012) and proposing the idea. While Dick is a man of definitive ideas and principles, he's not one to pontificate.

He's serious but doesn't take himself too seriously. He's proud of what he's accomplished, but it hadn't really occurred to him that anyone else would be interested in hearing about it.

Mark Wolf, a journalist who loves high school basketball enough to serve as an assistant coach at Columbine High School for 15 years, had to work hard at convincing Dick to write the book. He succeeded only by making Dick realize a book would "provide a platform for the values he wanted to convey, both in the game and in life."

I first knew Mark when he was just out of college and covering high school sports, a job he approached with the same kind of enthusiasm that a young Dick Katte brought to teaching math and coaching high school athletes. I got to know Mark even better when he entered a team in the first annual June Plastic Classic, a tournament conducted by the Colorado Whiffleball Federation, which I founded in 1975 and ran with a plastic fist as Commissioner for 34 years. Mark played in 17 CWF tournaments as the playing general manager for the Terrors, for which his sons Matt and Mike eventually starred. I can't think of any more impressive credentials than "journalist/basketball coach/whiffleball legend" for someone to document the life and times of Dick Katte.

Legends can be intimidating to the average man. If you look only at the statistics — the longevity, the wins, the state titles, the teaching mastery — you might think that Dick Katte is the kind of man who would make you feel inferior, act as reminder of all that you didn't accomplish.

On the contrary, spending time with Dick, which is what this book allows the reader to do, elevates you, makes you feel like you can be a better person.

What I love about Dick is his humanity. And his christianity, which I spell with a small "C," as he never would. I have a life-long distrust of "Christians" who aren't Christian, people whose talk doesn't mirror their actions. I trust Dick because his actions really do reflect his words.

Dick is always doing good things for other people, but he doesn't talk about it. If you sit down to socialize with him, you get up an hour later feeling good about yourself and concluding that the greatest living coach in Colorado is just a regular guy.

He may be a little more accomplished, a little more organized than you. Probably he's a little bit better person. But you don't mind. He brings you up with him, never steps on you on the way up.

There are many things I admire, even envy, about Dick Katte.

- Despite being one of the greatest basketball coaches in history, he can walk through an airport or eat in a restaurant without (generally) being recognized or bothered for an autograph.

- He's been married to the same woman for 55 years. Every bio on a person of note throws in something about a life-long marriage (regardless of how miserable) as proof of that person's loyalty, character, fidelity, etc. But if you've ever met Lorraine you immediately recognize her as someone worth being married to for 55 years. A truly great marriage is as rare a feat as winning 876 basketball games, and on a day-to-day basis, infinitely more satisfying and valuable. Lorraine has to comprise at least 50% of the formula for Dick's success.

- He's a competitor who understands competition. Don't for a minute think that Dick Katte is some Sunday school teacher whose locker room bulletin board has a sign on it, saying, "It's not whether you win or lose, it's how you play the game." People who win most of the time, win because they fiercely want to and know what it takes to win. And they hate losing, probably more than they love winning. Playing games without keeping score is a general waste of time and Dick Katte's not a guy who wastes time.

- He was an outstanding football referee (side judge, actually). There aren't many coaches who can make the transition between the clipboard and the whistle, but Dick went from the football field to the basketball bench for 26 years and excelled at both. Officials, like coaches, are special people and the heart of the games we play.

- He loved teaching math as much as he loved coaching basketball. People who truly love their jobs are uncommon. People who love their jobs and have great marriages are even more rare.

- He's not a big shot. He'll talk to anyone, from young coaches to his occasional golfing partner Rudy Carey, Denver East's long-time hoops maven.

- He always had time for the media and gets a kick out of seeing his name in the paper.

- He has an extended family of thousands of former students and players who genuinely love him.

- He can laugh at himself. When he's on one of his daily daybreak walks, I doubt that he spends much time thinking of himself as "The Great Basketball Coach." He's a humble man, and his lowly position in God's universe is the image that surrounds that solitary walk.

Enjoy the opportunity to be part of Dick Katte's universe so artfully presented by a talented writer and a fellow coach.

Bob Ottewill

Denver

March 21, 2014

Bob Ottewill is a writer for Mile High Sports Magazine and retired in 2002 after 30 years with the Colorado High School Activities Association."

A Note to Readers

This book is based on original research and interviews con
ducted with Dick Katte over the past two years. The first
chapter of this book, originally published in *Mile High Sports
Magazine,* is by Mark Wolf. The remainder of the book is in
Dick Katte's voice. When quotes are used to augment the nar-
rative, they are from interviews conducted by Wolf, or from
public events.

Male pronouns are used because Dick Katte coached boys
for 52 years but the basketball techniques and instruction apply equally to boys and girls..

Katte's iconic pose with hands behind his head with his longtime assistant and eventual successor Ray Van Heukelem beside him. Many have tried to interpret exactly what the pose conveys but not even he is certain. (Photo by Steve Vriesman)

Chapter 1: A Perfect Ending to a Legendary Career

The coach was up early as usual on the morning of The Last Game. He walked along the path of the Historic Arkansas Riverwalk of Pueblo, which follows the water through several blocks of downtown.

The Arkansas River seems ageless. It is vital and nourishing to what it encounters, much like Dick Katte.

For 48 years, Katte, 75, has been the head basketball coach at Denver Christian High School. As this day dawned, he had won 875 games and lost just 233; seven times his teams have won state championships and only twice have they lost more games than they won.

His current team is undefeated, 25-0, with only the State 2A Championship game remaining, a few miles away at the Colorado State Fair Grounds Events Center. History infused this game with far more drama and irony than any fiction writer could dare.

This night's opponent, in Katte's last game, is Limon, the same team against which he began his coaching career.

The stakes were far smaller that chilly Dec. 4, 1964, when Katte took his Crusaders to Limon. Temperatures were in the 20s as Denver Christian rode an 18-point second quarter to a 45-42 victory, No. 1 on a list that would come to dominate Colorado's schoolboy coaching records.

Elsewhere that same day in '64, the FBI arrested 21 people suspected in the lynching deaths of three civil rights workers in Mississippi in what became known as the Mississippi Burning case. The Soviet Union charged U.S. President Lyndon Johnson was planning to escalate military action against North Vietnam and Laos. A bench-clearing brawl erupted in the final minute of the basketball game between the University of

Colorado and the University of Denver. Sunday turkey dinner was 99 cents at Hested's department store. And none of the 20 movie theaters advertised on the front page of the *Rocky Mountain News* entertainment listings are still in business.

Katte is the most-honored high school coach in Colorado history with numerous Coach of the Year awards, Hall of Fame inductions and being the first recipient of the Dave Sanders Award which was given in memory of the Columbine teacher and basketball coach who was killed while trying to help students escape during the 1999 school shootings.

As he walks along the paved thoroughfare beside the Arkansas River, past stores and restaurants that are yet to open, the final piece of Dick Katte's basketball legacy remains to be determined.

It has been a long week and it will be a long day.

THE BUILDUP

Dick Katte calculates he has conducted somewhere in the neighborhood of 3,000 practices, virtually all of them in the Denver Christian gymnasium named for him.

"See, it wasn't a setup," he calls to a visitor on the Monday of The Last Week. The previous day's *Denver Post* featured a large picture of Katte pushing a broom across the hardwood floor, and here he was sweeping the floor as his players trickled in and snatched balls off a rack beside the court.

Few of those practices have been more scrutinized than the ones of these last few weeks since he announced he was going to retire at season's end. He has worn microphones for several TV stations, had writers eavesdropping, and both video and still photographers capturing his every move.

It is impossible to deflect the attention, so he urges his team to embrace it.

"Sorry about the distractions. Channel 7 is coming tomorrow. Thought you looked good on TV the other night. For as much as I apologize to you, how many high school kids get all of this? Savor the moment," he said as he gathered his players before practice.

Other than basic shooting drills and working on their specific sets, the Crusaders rarely run the same drill twice during the week.

"I try never to make my practices predictable, even at my age. There are some basic things you can never skip," he said. "We try to give it a little variety. I have to remind myself not to over-coach. We all think, 'We're in the tournament and it's all about the coaching. We have to add this and add that.' I don't think that's true. Just make sure they can do the things that are good to us, and defense has been good to us."

He is a stickler for the details that could make the difference between being a champion and being just another team that came pretty close.

"Don't be flat-footed. Make your dribble take you somewhere. You went like this [stretching out his arm] instead of doing that [stepping hard into a ballhandler's path]. Each mistake must be corrected. Go straight up and straight down."

When too many free throws clank off the rim, Katte lines his team on the baseline for a trio of down-and-back sprints.

Watching him run practice, it's nearly impossible to believe he is 75 years old. Katte carries himself with an athlete's easy grace, walks with urgency, striding to the middle of the free throw line when he needs to direct or correct.

"Being around young people helps you think young and stay young," he said. So does a daily two-mile walk at 5:30 a.m. (When he was still working full time, he walked at 4:30 AM.)

"It's quiet. You can really think, meditate."

All week, he emphasized what they have accomplished and what remains to be gained.

"It's our mission as coaches to get you to this point. Now, it's in your hands. Focus. Get yourselves ready. Get some rest. Three nights in a row, we've never done that. You're in a good spot," he told his team on Monday.

Monday and Tuesday's practices were productive, but the intensity dimmed at the end. Wednesday, The Last Practice, was nearly flawless. Katte set the tone in his pre-practice talk.

"This is going to be a memorable weekend. I give you this reminder: The season proves you were the best team in 2A basketball, but the best team doesn't always win. I've had teams that were the best and didn't win and teams that weren't the best and did. Most of the time it's focus and intensity."

This is one of his favorite teams, not just for what they have accomplished, but how. They are balanced, unselfish, hard-working, tenacious defensively. He thinks they are ready, but they are high school kids and he has brought what he believed was the best team in the state to this level before and seen them falter.

At practice's end, he sent his team away with perspective about what the rest of the week held.

"All this hoopla the last two weeks, I'm going to guess there hasn't been a high school team to get as much coverage as you have. For all of you, that means the big stage in Pueblo is going to be nothing. Our only focus is tomorrow. We want to go out and be ready to play. We're standing on the verge of greatness."

And, a familiar exhortation: "Play hard, do your best, be a good teammate and leave the rest to God."

For the last time in this gym, the players and coaches put their hands together overhead and broke The Last Practice with a communal chant: "Great."

And just like that, it was over.

"I did think about that a little bit," said Katte. "I thought, 'Why am I giving this up? I enjoy this.'"

874

Riley Herren, the Crusaders' pace-pushing point guard and defensive standout, sensed his team was tight: "It seemed like everyone was nervous at the beginning of the day."

From the outset against a Sanford team that had put up 102 points in a game earlier in the season, the Crusaders were dogged defensively, helping, sliding and closing out, but over-eager on offense, rushing possessions, missing good shots.

Katte's team gave up only seven points in the first half, yet scored just 18.

Katte seemed relatively unconcerned about what he was seeing: "Because they went so hard on defense, they were playing too fast on offense," he said.

Eventually his team settled down, stretched the lead and rolled to a 56-33 victory, but not without a scare.

Early in the second half, Crusaders star Austin LeFebre, a gifted 6-5 forward who is the best player in the 2A category and would be a force at any level, finished a fast-break layup but crumpled to the floor holding his right ankle. He was helped to the bench, but returned a few minutes later and played well the rest of the game, scoring a team-high 16 points.

Still, the injury was concerning. He was favoring it after the game and the fear was he would wake up with a painful, swollen ankle in the morning. Nobody needs this kind of drama with the two biggest games of the season looming within 48 hours.

875

Katte arranged for his team to have a shoot-around Friday morning at Widefield High School located between Colorado Springs and Pueblo. LeFebre's ankle appeared fine, but he was ushered into the school's modern and expansive training room, where trainer Bob Tim ("One of the best in the state," said Katte) examined him.

"It hurt this morning," LeFebre acknowledged.

Tim wrapped the ankle first with blue, then white tape and said he didn't think it would bother him.

After the Crusaders ran through a few drills in the spacious, old-style gymnasium, Katte talked about what they would expect from this night's opponent, rival Lutheran High School. Christian had defeated Lutheran twice this season, but the Lights' 16-9 record was misleading due to a number of tough games against class 3A competition.

"They've started out really strong against us in both games and Jonny Foote was the guy. I think he had their first 11 points in our gym and at Mullen he had 23. Coach (Andy) Draayer and I talked and I think we'll start with a box and one," said Katte.

Draayer, who was the class 3A Mr. Basketball for Christian in 2002, reminded the players to always be aware of Lutheran's screens whether they are in man-to-man or zone.

The most hopeful sign of the morning? LeFebre, whose family and friends wear "Dunking Dutchman" t-shirts, finished the workout with an emphatic slam.

Sitting next to his wife, Lorraine, who is rarely more than a short bounce pass from her husband during the tournament, and with other family members nearby, Katte watched Limon hand Resurrection Christian only its third loss of the season – the others were to Denver Christian – to advance to the title game. He sketched a couple of plays on his whiteboard; she pulled an iPad from her purse. As he got up to leave during halftime of the girls' semifinal, she gave him a soft pat on the back.

The Crusaders didn't shoot well, took too many outside shots and committed excessive turnovers as Lutheran jumped to an 11-8 lead after the first quarter, but then Christian began to look like the team they'd been all year.

With Katte more animated than usual on the bench, Lutheran scored just three points in the second quarter and Christian established a 20-14 halftime lead. It only got better. LeFebre's ankle seemed fine, but it was junior guard Alex Terpstra's night. He hit back-to-back corner jump shots; Chris Pranger made a precise bounce pass through Lutheran's zone for a LeFebre layup, and the Crusaders pulled away to a 55-39 victory and a chance to send their coach out with his eighth state title.

"Tonight, you just did it," Katte told his team. "You played the way I coach and I'm so thankful. You played with confidence. Every time there was a challenge, you responded. There's one left, let's not even think about it. Savor the moment."

LeFebre said his ankle "was feeling pretty good. We got the jitters out of us. We were all hyped up (the night before), but today we were just ready to play."

The players had resisted focusing too much on Katte's retirement.

"He wanted the focus to be on us. We wanted to put him out on a really good note."

876

It was a long day leading up to The Last Game. The shootaround was in a small gym with a linoleum floor and one basket lower than the other. The team checked out of the Marriott, drove through the Minnequa Business District, past Lupita's Mexican Restaurant and the Nunez Lounge, on their way to the arena.

"They're sitting up there watching basketball and getting nervous," Katte said, waving an arm towards his team a dozen or so rows up from where he and Lorraine occupied the first two seats of row I in the corner of the arena.

Katte's pregame talks are much more conversations with his players than recitations of points of emphasis and matchups.

"I think for a group like this, the journey is the destination. Think about that. More than that gold ball, all we went through together was our destination. Here we are at the climax, and I really want you to go out there and perform, show them what Denver Christian basketball is all about," he said.

He opened the floor for a discussion about his four Ps (pressure, poise, push and patience), then spoke of the woman to whom he has been married since Dwight Eisenhower was in the White House.

"I hope you all get a wife as good as mine; she kept these stats," he said, as he passed around charts on Limon.

From the tipoff, it all went their way. Herren passed ahead to LeFebre for a dunk. Chris Pranger converted a layup. Herren to LeFebre again for a layup. Terpstra drains a three. On the other end, steals, stops and misses. By the time Herren jump stopped at the free throw line and Connor Kroshus cut past him for an easy layup, the Crusaders' lead was 17-2.

Dick Katte's last game was going to be a waltz. It looked too easy, and it was.

Limon inched back, milking its possessions for good shots. The lead dwindled to 30-22 at halftime.

If these kids thought the last halftime speech Dick Katte would ever give them was going to be full of reassurance, they hadn't been paying attention. In their last game, they were letting him down.

"You played almost a perfect six minutes of team basketball and the last 10 minutes I saw selfishness, saw players hollering at each other. That's not the way we play. We're shooting shots we shouldn't shoot. Swing the ball, its much better to go inside out and shoot, not bomb from the outside. There is no discipline. You did it so perfectly, then all of a sudden you played into their hands and you didn't play the way we talked about," he said, less with rancor than disappointment. "We have at least four offensive fouls. Somehow, you have to get a little smarter. You have to pull up and use the blackboard."

The storybook version would be that the Crusaders righted themselves and regained control early in the second half. But they didn't. Limon's confidence grew. They made shots and bumped Christian's cutters off their paths. The lead dwindled to a single point when Kroshus was fouled underneath. He had two shots and missed them both. Fifteen seconds later, Limon's Chandler Dobe hit a step-back jumper from the baseline and Limon owned a 45-44 lead.

At the most dangerous moment of the season, with Limon streaking and Christian reeling, the Crusaders pushed the ball up-court and Kroshus caught it on the left sideline.

You need to know this about Connor Kroshus: He's a 45 percent shooter, averaging more than one three-pointer per game and Christian's second-leading rebounder. However, this had not been a good shooting week for him. He was one-for-seven from three-point range against Sanford and Lutheran, and had tossed up a couple of airballs.

The Events Center can be a tough place to shoot. A black curtain hangs behind one end of the court and a trio of three-point lines (high school, college, pro) ring the perimeter.

While Kroshus' teammates were standing in a breezeway waiting to take the court before the championship game, he was in the hallway, flipping the ball off his fingertips against a concrete arena wall just above an exit sign.

The last time he'd touched the ball in the state championship game he had missed a pair of free throws.

Still, there are moments when preparation, opportunity and confidence conspire to intersect at the perfect time. Athletes sense them, which is why Connor Kroshus squared to the basket and lofted a shot from behind the correct three-point line that nestled into the net to give the Crusaders a 47-45 advantage.

As painstakingly as Limon had erased their lead, the Crusaders had dramatically regained it. The student section behind Christian's bench, many of the fans equipped with Katte facemasks, erupted. The coach raised his hands, exhorting defense.

Limon missed. Herren penetrated, found Kroshus on the baseline for a layup and a four-point lead. Limon cut it to two late and some missed Crusader free throws extended the drama until Kroshus hit the first of two free throws with 1.8 seconds left for the final 54-50 score.

His players lifted Katte aloft and carried him to the sideline.

After celebrating, they made their way to the locker room for the last time where the coach led his team in prayer.

"God, it was just great to play before all these people, to be a force that unified them for Denver Christian. These guys showed their heart, their spirit, their love for one another and for me as their coach, I thank you for that. Bless each one of us as we go on our way now for life after basketball. I pray that the rest of the year may be a good one for all of us. To Your name be the glory, in Jesus name. A-MEN."

In the 1,109th game of his career, Dick Katte coached his team literally until the last second. A guy with a clipboard can't ask for much more.

"It doesn't get any better than that. They challenged you. We had them down and they didn't go away," he said. "If I was going to go out, it was just great to finish it with you. Thank you. We're going to celebrate in a lot of different ways, but this was really satisfying. In the bottom of your heart, this

2012 Champions: Back row from left, Austin LeFebre, Connor Kroshus,
Austin Hart, Robert Parker, Coach Katte, Tate Kastens, Chris Pranger, Alex
Terpstra, Jared Van Dyke. Front row from left, Josh Carter, Riley Herren,
Rafael Luna, Mason Hofer, Forrest Sanderson (Photo by Lifetouch National
School Studios)

Coach Katte gets a ride on the shoulders of his last team after winning the 2012
state championship in his final game. (Photo by The Pueblo Chieftain)

Dick and Lorraine Katte hold the championship trophy after Dick's last game.

Members of the Blue Crew root for their team during the 2012 state tournament. (Photo by Alan Hart)

is what you dreamed of. Now you did it. Without any losses. Wow."

For his part, Kroshus said he never hesitated to take the game-changing shot.

"Not at all. I was going up. By the third day, you get adapted to (the shooting background). Today in warm-ups, they had the right distance," he said.

Just curious; did he miss that last free throw on purpose to run out the clock?

"You could say that," he said with a wry grin.

The Crusaders crowd cheered each player as he left the locker room and roared when Katte emerged. After the well-wishers trickled away, the coach, his wife and their son, Keith, who played on Christian's last undefeated team in 1978, walked across a dark parking lot.

The coach slid the big gold ball trophy into the back seat of his car, and he and Lorraine drove away with The Last Game in their rearview mirror.

(Originally published in the February 2013 edition of Mile High Sports Magazine. Reprinted by permission.)

Chapter 2: Growing Up in Sheboygan

I was raised in a room with a view. Lighthouse Court on the east side of Sheboygan in Wisconsin was then, as now, a quiet, shady street less than two blocks from Lake Michigan and, as the name implies, within sight of a lighthouse.

When I was born on June 12, 1936, the nation was beginning to yawn itself out of the Great Depression, although national unemployment was nearly 17 percent. Our house was one of nearly 13,000 homes in Sheboygan, whose population was nudging up to 40,000.

My grandparents on my father's side came from the Netherlands. My parents, Dan and Mary, raised three boys and three girls in their two-story house near the end of Lighthouse Court. I was the first-born, and I had a room with a porch on the second floor facing the street. When it was hot in the house, the porch was often a good place to catch a cool breeze off the lake.

We were poor, but we always had good food and a nice warm house. Dad took his bike to work at the American Chair Company factory (we had no car) and worked 8 to 10 hours every day. He eventually started a little upholstery business in his basement where he worked on nights and weekends while continuing his job at the factory. My job was to go with him to pick up chairs and couches and bring them to the basement. He would let me take the old material off, but never let me put things back together. He was an excellent upholsterer and had many gracious customers in town.

American Chair had operated in Sheboygan since 1888 and was the second largest player in the city's thriving furniture industry until April 19, 1982 when a boiler exploded. As reported by the *Shebyogan Press*, the resulting fire injured nine

Dick and his parents in Sheboygan.

people and gutted the four-story wooden factory which was located near the Sheboygan River less than two miles from our home.

My parents were godly people with very strong values. Dad was a very hard worker who loved his family. I can remember my mother and dad taking a vacation only once while I lived at home. He was always busy providing, and Mom was his helpmate. Mom always prepared good meals, baked bread and pastries, and she received joy from cooking and baking for us even though times were hard. On Mondays and Thursdays she did a huge wash using a wringer washer and hung the wash outside on the lines even when it was very cold. Everything had to be ironed—even the sheets! She also took in ironing from a neighbor, and later worked for that family doing housework. Mom took the youngest of the four children (3 months old) into our home and cared for her for a couple of years after their mother died suddenly from a brain aneurysm.

There were about a dozen boys in our neighborhood, and there was a vacant lot in the area where we played ball. I was the youngest boy in the group. We did some fun things and probably some naughty things too. In those days nothing was organized, but we played games like kick the can and lots of ball games. Being the youngest helped me and hurt me. Sometimes I was the victim of the roughhousing kids do, but it helped me to hold my own against older kids.

Vollrath Park was a couple of blocks from our house. It had lighted tennis courts even back then as well as some hills that provided excellent sledding.

When I was 16, my dad bought a 1948 Chevrolet, so he could take the car to work at the factory, and our family had more freedom to go places. Before we had a car, when my sister Jan needed a tonsillectomy, Dad took her to the hospital on his bicycle.

The church has been a major influence in my life since childhood, and my family was a member of the Christian Reformed Church. Our family attended Sunday morning and Sunday evening services at First Christian Reformed Church, a few blocks from our house. We usually walked to church, and my uncle would take us home in his car before we had our own. Back then the church was bustling. During the years I was at home in Sheboygan, the church grew from 191 to 270 families and 1,074 members.

Our church sent 132 young men to serve in World War II. Of the 26 men from Sheboygan killed in the war, two were from our church: PFC Lester Vander Weele, who was killed in 1942, and Marvin TeWinkel, who perished in 1945. A banner was hung in the front of church with a blue star for each member in the armed services and a gold star for those who had lost their lives. I remember how solemn it was being in church when it was announced that someone was missing or killed in action. When the war was over in 1945, I remember riding my tricycle down the alley, and I pounded on a pan with a big stick to make a lot of noise. The neighbors came out into the streets banging on pots and pans to celebrate the victory! There were sirens and cars were honking their horns in the town.

As is the case with many children, embracing my family's religion took some time. There were many rigid expectations in the church. Growing up as I did, discipline meant punishment and restrictions. Today I believe discipline is knowing what you can do and when you can do it. The church has always been a big part of my life, and some of those teachings are a part of me today.

A lot of kids back then had part-time jobs to help the family's finances. When I was in fifth grade I would rise at 4 a.m. to work on a milk delivery truck. The driver would stop in front of each house on the route, and I would jump off the truck and put the milk in the boxes on the porch.

I also delivered *The Sheboygan Press*, which was then an afternoon paper, to 50-plus customers every day on my bicycle. Those jobs were so important to my family to help support the six children. When I played high school sports, my dad would go to the *Sheboygan Press* to pick up my papers and then drop them off at the high school so I could deliver them on my bike after I finished practice.

Despite its size, Sheboygan was not without professional sports. In 1949 the Sheboygan Red Skins became a charter member of the National Basketball Association. Though the franchise lasted only a single NBA season and played in the tiny Municipal Armory, the team had a flash of glory by defeating the defending champion Minneapolis Lakers (later the L.A. Lakers) with Hall of Fame center George Mikan.

I did get to go to a few games. The "under twelve" group always sat behind the baskets in that old armory. When I got to high school we played our big rivalry game against Sheboygan Central (now Sheboygan South) in that Armory.

My dad was a big baseball fan, and he hit countless ground balls to me in our wide side yard. Whenever he was working downstairs, a radio was on, and he listened to his favorite announcer, Jack Brickhouse, describe Chicago Cubs games. For my tenth birthday dad took me on a train to Chicago for a Cubs game. We stayed overnight in nearby hotel and went to Wrigley Field to watch as the Cubs of Stan Hack, Andy Pafko, and Phil Cavarretta faced the eventual World Series Champions St. Louis Cardinals, whose lineup featured Stan Musial, Enos Slaughter, Red Schoendist, Whitcy Kurowski, and Marty Marion.

My dad always kept a scorecard, and I think I still have the one from that game. I don't think any boy ever forgets his first major league game, and I was in awe watching those players play in that park. Later when we had our own car, we went to Chicago for other games during the Fourth of July week— the only time dad took vacation. If the Cubs weren't in town we would go see the White Sox.

My elementary school years were at the Sheboygan Christian School, which was for children of the Christian Reformed Church. By the time I was in high school, I was among the bigger boys in my class and a promising athlete. Because there was no Christian high school, I attended Sheboygan North, a prominent city school whose athletic teams competed regularly against Green Bay and Appleton schools in one of the state's better conferences.

Sheboygan North, now Urban Middle School (the new North High School is next door), opened in 1938 and is the kind of school that used to be built in this country. It stands three stories high, in contrast to today's sprawling ranch-style educational edifices. I probably didn't appreciate it at the time, but art deco highlights are all over the school, staircases are wide with skylights above them and bordered by thick wood railings. The auditorium seats over 1,000 people, and you can climb up to the bell tower.

Dad encouraged me to play sports, but he didn't want me to play football — so I had to convince my mother to sign the permission papers. I made the Golden Raiders' varsity football team as a sophomore, and my first game had a lasting impact on the way I would eventually coach my own players.

We played East Green Bay at City Field where the Packers played, and at halftime we were down 41-0. Our coach was not very kind in the way he belittled us and the way he degraded us. I have disliked Green Bay ever since the humiliation I endured in that locker room. To this day I can never cheer for the Packers. It reminds me how impressionable young people are and that some of that treatment stays with a person forever.

By the time I was a senior I was an all-conference lineman and also kicked extra points. I can remember how proud my little brother was of me, and he was waiting for me on the steps when I came home to show me the article in the newspaper about me. In those days football helmets did not have facemasks. I also played tuba in the band, and, like a lot of my friends, I walked a mile and a half to my home for lunch where my mother would have lunch waiting for me.

My best sport was baseball and I was also able to play it in college.

When I was chosen to play in a high school baseball all-star game, I couldn't participate because the game was on Sunday. I considered slipping away and playing under an assumed name but quickly thought better of it.

It's ironic that I wound up as a basketball coach because that was by far my worst sport. I was a starter the first half of my senior season in basketball, but we didn't win many games. The coach called the seniors in and said, "We're going to build for the future, and you four aren't going to play anymore."

That was a bitter pill to swallow. I was used to being a starter in football and baseball, and here I was sitting on the bench as a senior. In hindsight it may have helped me learn by observing the game, but I didn't feel that way at the time. At least when I have told players who weren't playing much that I understood what they were going through, I could tell them from my own experience.

We didn't have much money, but there was no doubt I was going to go college, and in my father's mind there was no question about where I was going! I didn't give much serious thought to what kind of career I wanted to pursue, but I do remember telling an eighth grade teacher that I thought teaching might be a good career.

I had offers to play football at Montana State and Stetson, and an assistant principal at Sheboygan Central, who had been a military officer and was a graduate of West Point, assured me I could go there.

However, my dad said I was going to Calvin College in Grand Rapids, Michigan. Calvin was affiliated with the Christian Reformed Church. I fought it and believed I could thrive at a larger school, but he didn't waver. It was important in those days for the church members to promote their own into Christian schools and Christian colleges, and I was raised to be obedient to my parents so off to Calvin I went.

Tuition was less than $200 a semester, and it was based on how great the distance was to the college. Grand Rapids was across Lake Michigan from Sheboygan (120 miles), but it was an eight-hour, 350-mile trip around Lake Michigan to get there so I really paid more than I should have! Each summer I found a job near my home. Most of them were less than desirable, but I needed them to pay my tuition.

Calvin College, named for John Calvin, had about 1,400 students when I enrolled; today's enrollment is more than 4,000. The academics were rigorous, and classes were taught from a Christian perspective. The school's mission statement emphasizes it "has grown out of a noble vision: to shape hearts and minds for Christian living and to send out agents of renewal and reconciliation in God's Kingdom."

Two veteran teachers at Calvin became strong influences on my future: math teacher John Tuls and physical education teacher Barney Steen. Math was my major, and John Tuls had high expectations and taught the subject in a very structured and understandable way that impressed me. Barney Steen was the head of the PE department and my baseball coach. He mentored me, and gave me a lot of privileges and opportunities.

Going to Calvin was a growth experience and not without its growing pains. I was a well-known guy in high school, and all of a sudden it was "Dick Who?" My first two months there

I was kind of living in the past — not enjoying college, just thinking how good it had been in high school.

I worked part-time taking orders at general merchandise wholesaler W.J. Dykstra in Grand Rapids to help pay tuition. I studied math and spent a lot of time hanging around the basketball team—a relationship that would have an impact on my life several decades later. I began to think more and more about teaching and coaching.

But it was a scavenger hunt that changed my life.

Early in my sophomore year, Lorraine Stap, a freshman who had come to Calvin from her family's farm near Lynden, Washington, half a mile from the Canadian border, needed a date for her guild house's social event during "twirp week" at Calvin. (Twirp week was when the woman is required to pay.)

Lorraine was a nursing student who lived in a guild house with 10 freshmen girls who had to share one bathroom. One of her roommates urged her to call a friend of hers to ask him to accompany her on a scavenger hunt for a guild house social.

I didn't know whom I was talking to, but my roommate said, "Go ahead." The next day I was in the library, and my roommate pointed Lorraine out to me and said, "That's whom you're going with."

I decided I had made a pretty good decision. It took me a couple weeks to get enough courage to have another date, but by the end of her freshman year we were a couple. I do remember worrying that somebody in nurses training who was around doctors all the time wouldn't want to be with a poor college kid.

Our interests were completely different. She gravitated more to art, plays and classical music. She didn't know much about sports. I took her to the first college football game she ever saw — Michigan vs. Navy at Ann Arbor in 1958. She was shocked when she walked into that huge stadium!

Almost everything at Calvin College was an integration of academics from a Christian perspective. Spending time with Lorraine and not as much time with the boys had a real influence on me. After her first year at Calvin, she lived in the

Dick and Lorraine prepare for homecoming at Calvin College.

nurses' lodge at the hospital. I didn't have a car then, so we did a lot of walking on our dates.

When I graduated in 1958, I travelled to Lynden to ask Lorraine's father for her hand. I was simultaneously impressed by the beauty of the land in Washington and how her family welcomed a city slicker who knew nothing of the ways of farmers.

I had graduated in June and became a teaching assistant at Calvin. She graduated the following September and became a nurse at Blodgett Hospital in Grand Rapids.

We were married the following July 3. It was during the week that my father had vacation. The factory where he worked closed for vacation the week of the Fourth. My entire family—mom, dad and five siblings—drove more than 2,000 miles from Sheboygan to Lynden, Washington in the family's 1952 Impala.

After we were married we moved to Bloomington, Indiana. Lorraine worked as a nurse while I attended graduate school at Indiana University and earned a Master's Degree in Education.

I was hoping to return to Calvin College as a teacher and coach with my masters degree, but when no suitable openings arose, I applied to three Christian high schools: one in California, one in Michigan and one at the corner of Pearl Street and Evans Avenue in Denver,which was to become my professional home for the next 52 years.

Chapter 3: Finding a Home at Denver Christian

As it turned out, this was an easy choice. Denver Christian was affiliated with the Christian Reformed Church just like Calvin College. It was supported by tuition paying families. Both Lorraine and I had been raised in the Christian Reformed faith; Lorraine attended Christian schools through high school in Lynden, WA, and I attended Sheboygan Christian through eighth grade. We met at Calvin College in Grand Rapids, MI.

When I graduated from Indiana University, a mentor of mine at Indiana said he could get me a job at Western Michigan University High School, but a small school in central Denver, located relatively equidistant from my parents in Wisconsin and Lorraine's in Washington, seemed to be where we belonged. Denver Christian was founded in 1916 in a single building and since has grown to three campuses. When I was hired in 1960, it had more than 180 students in grades 7-12. The journey from Bloomington to Denver was uneventful—except that we arrived three weeks ahead of our furniture. A neighbor across from our rented house graciously helped out with a few basics until our belongings arrived. Lorraine was expecting our first child; Keith was born 10 weeks after we arrived in Denver.

Denver Christian paid me $3,200 to teach four math courses and three physical education classes, plus an additional $200 because I was married, as was the custom in that era. I earned another $200 for coaching junior varsity basketball and track. By comparison, you could buy a new Chevrolet Corvair for $2,238 and gasoline was about 25 cents per gallon.

I loved mathematics, and it turned out to be a timely and fortuitous career choice. The nation was still suffering an inferiority complex that the Soviets had beaten us into space with the 1957 launch of Sputnik, and the public clamored for an increased emphasis on math and science teaching. This spurred America to action in the space race.

I attended seven intensive summer mathematics institutes for teachers, financed by the National Science Foundation, and earned a second Master's Degree in Mathematics from Utah State University in 1972. An added benefit was sharing experiences and learning strategies with other math teachers from around the country. The experience made me an even stronger advocate for math education and prompted me to give up the physical education aspect of my teaching career.

I remember how hard I worked in preparation for those first classes at Denver Christian. I didn't want to walk into class unprepared and just wing it. As I look back, that attention to detail and readiness set the stage for lessons of preparation I would use as a coach and teacher throughout my career.

I coached several sports to help out the school and to make a little extra money, but I quickly saw the rewards of the relationships a young coach can forge with high school students. The rapport you develop with young people has much more to do with their success than all the Xs and Os you teach.

Basketball was already an important part of the school and community culture by the time I arrived. Denver Christian's teams were perennially successful playing an independent schedule against other private schools as well as games against public schools like Limon, Castle Rock and Idaho Springs.

Coach Ray Lucht's varsity team was undefeated during my first season as junior varsity coach and held their own in a scrimmage against George Washington's Patriots, who would go on to capture Colorado's big-school state championship.

When I began at Denver Christian, it was almost exclusively comprised of young people of families of the Christian Reformed Church many of whom lived in South Denver. Today, the student body represents more than 170 different Christian churches.

The heritage of the Christian Reformed Church is Dutch, and over the years those families have provided Denver Christian with a stream of tall, blond, big-boned boys who gravitated to basketball. Several of them moved on to play at Calvin College, the denomination's flagship educational institution, whose perennially strong program has produced a pair of NCAA Division III basketball championships.

"It was predominantly a neighborhood school, and you had that cradle-to-the-grave dedication. My dad went to Denver Christian up through eighth grade before they had a high school," recalls Ray Van Heukelem, whose association with Katte began that year and lasted more than five decades as a student, player, assistant coach, colleague and eventual successor—who won a state championship his first season.

"Basketball was the only big sport when I was growing up. When they had that undefeated team in 1961 I would go over and watch them play. I knew all those players."

Ray was a seventh grader when I first met him as a student in one of my physical education classes.

"He walked in, and I swear his calves were bigger than his thighs," he said. "He was a no-nonsense, intimidating PE teacher to a bunch of junior high boys. But he was very different as a math teacher, a whole lot more caring and concerned and wanting to work with us one-on-one."

I became the head coach when Ray was beginning his junior year.

"He was very demanding," said Van Heukelem. "It was his way or no way. Back in those days, a coach told you something and it was so because he said so. I remember how hard we tried to play for him. It was very competitive. Basketball was our whole world. You knew from the time you were in seventh grade that you had to try out, and if you didn't want to get cut you had to be practicing all the time. There weren't those other distractions. Young people today have so many other outlets that they don't fight for survival in sports anymore."

"He brought a lot of football mentality into the basketball arena: playing tough, playing hard, defense first. We really had to work. We trusted that he knew what he was doing. He had a knack for going out and finding answers, and I knew he was getting good quality direction about basketball from coaches

like Guy Gibbs (the legendary coach at Regis High School) and Irv Brown (then a coach at Arvada High School).

My first game as a head coach was at home against Limon. Two things were memorable: Limon just happened to be the defending class C State Champion, and we won, 45-42.

The second game I coached was sobering. Westminster High School, a school from the largest state classification, drilled the Crusaders 93-54. I confided to Lorraine that I wasn't sure I was cut out to be a basketball coach.

"I remember that game very well. Don Schneider was a great player for us when I was a junior. We went over to play Westminster. They were a top team, knew about Don and put a box and one on him and completely bottled him up. Dick didn't know what to do about it and was frustrated. His response was to do a lot of research and make himself into a more knowledgeable coach," recalled Van Heukelem.

I took those losses very personally in my early coaching years. I would build up the players but would come home, be very quiet, and I did not want to talk after a loss. My wife was very understanding, and with time my quiet demeanor after losses improved.

Later in the season we played Limon again at Limon. Limon's old gym was a bandbox, much like many small town gyms of that era. The sidelines were only a foot or so from the wall, and a dotted line was painted three feet from the out-of-bounds line to delineate where a defender could stand during a throw-in.

In the second half, Van Heukelem stepped on the dotted line while saving the ball from going out of bounds, but the official blew his whistle, called him out of bounds and awarded the ball to Limon.

I stood up, said, "No way," and the whistle blew again. I had my first technical!

"I thought, 'this guy's all right. He's going to stand up for me'," said Van Heukelem. "He kept me from saying anything to the official. It was like, 'OK, coach has got this.'"

My memory says there were only six other technicals on me in my 48-year varsity career. One was when I had a wrong number in the scorebook.

A year after becoming Christian's head basketball coach, I added athletic director's duties as well as becoming the head baseball coach. Lacking football, DC started soccer as a fall sport and added wrestling the next year. The impetus behind the expansion was to lay the groundwork for entrée into the "official" world of Colorado high school sports.

Denver Christian and the state's other private schools lived in a tent city outside the walled fortress of the Colorado High School Activities Association. When our seasons were finished, the public schools geared up for state tournaments that received generous coverage in both of Denver's then-thriving daily newspapers. Some of the parochial teams could have competed at the highest level of their classifications in the tournaments, but even the best ones were relegated to the athletic netherworld of "What if ...".

Take our "unofficial and uncrowned state championship team of 1966-67" for example. After going 14-5 and 16-5 in our first two seasons, we returned several key players from those teams who formed the nucleus of a squad that would make the state's basketball establishment sit up and take notice.

Jeff Mains was the star of that team and his heroics helped us win five games with crucial shots in the waning minute. The most memorable was his buzzer-beater from the corner, which capped a five-point Crusader comeback in the last 28 seconds against Sheridan.

Eldon Likkel was another senior leader on the team. His parents had recently separated.

"It was very unusual in our school, a church school, for a kid not to have a two-parent family," said Likkel. "I had a great mother, but I was sensitive to it in some situations."

I was only 10 years older than Eldon, more like a big brother age-wise, but I told him I knew he was going to need a father figure and that I had some very high expectations of him and wanted him to trust me as his mentor. Another senior leader and a significant contributor was Glenn Dykstra who fit perfectly the description of Denver Christian players—tall, blond, and raw boned.

We began our season by winning our first three games, and then we lost a tough two-point game to Westminster.

"They were good, but I thought we were better," recalled Mains. "We missed a lot of layups and wound up losing to a team we shouldn't have lost to."

I was disappointed by the effort and execution we displayed and I decided to do something to get their attention. I told them that by Tuesday they were to report to practice with their hair cut as short as my crew cut as a way to renew their commitment. It's not as if their hair was falling into their eyes or anything, it just draped over their ears and foreheads. They weren't very happy about it, but the neighborhood barbers did very good business on Monday.

"We were going to gulp hard, but we were going to do what he said," said Mains.

A week later, Jeff had back-to-back games of 27 and 25 points and the Denver Post selected him as the high school "Player of the Week."

"They took my picture with that terrible haircut," he said.

The point wasn't the length or the style of their hair. In fact, I came to terms with longer hairstyles over the years. What I wanted to do was develop a feeling of solidarity into a group that I knew was going to be good but had the potential to be great with increased commitment and trust.

I don't know if the haircut incident had much to do with it, but they ran the table the rest of the season and finished 20-1.

"We played competition that was way over our head, a lot of AAA (then the state's largest classification) schools," said Likkel, a versatile and valuable starter who ranked second in scoring, third in rebounding, and was a strong defender.

"I passed the ball to Jeff a lot. I probably would have the school record for assists if we'd kept track of them. Coach just put me in a position to be successful. He didn't ask me to do more than I was capable of doing.

"He made us believe that if we just worked hard and dedicated ourselves, we could accomplish almost anything. His

best quality as a coach was his ability to adjust to and play the style of basketball that accommodated the style of the players he had. He would change his system to fit the players he had. He's had run-and-gun teams, he's had half-court teams, and he was able to get the most out of everybody. He'd say, 'This is what you're good at and this is what you need to do for the team.' He was demanding but he made you believe there wasn't anything you couldn't do."

Mains concurred. "He made you work. He never tried to have you just be good, he wanted you to push yourself to take the next step. If you were one of the better players he expected you to lead the team. It was a hard work ethic but fun while we did it. He wanted you to be so focused that you could do what you needed to do but didn't want you to be at odds with another player. He just wanted you to be better."

One of the strongest messages I tried to convey to my players was that 'You play like you practice.' You never know if your players take things like that to heart but one night Jeff inadvertently provided the perfect example. He had picked up a habit during practice scrimmages of not passing the ball in-bounds but instead merely dribbling it up the floor. Then he did it in a game.

Jeff remembers, "I think we were behind by a couple of points, and I just dribbled the ball to half-court without passing it in. Thanks heavens the referee didn't realize what I had done. Coach just looked at me like, 'what are you doing?' "

From the beginning I always believed that my teams got better by playing against the best competition, and we scheduled scrimmages against the state's best programs, regardless of enrollment. The week after George Washington handed rival Thomas Jefferson its only loss of the season, we went nose-to-nose with GW in a midweek scrimmage.

"We thought we won by one or two points. GW might remember it the other way," said Mains, "but when we had a chance to listen to the state tournament games on the radio we knew those players on all levels and knew we'd been successful against them."

Not a lot of people know this but our last game of the season against Lutheran was quite dramatic for a couple of reasons.

Jeff Mains' mother, Betty, was epileptic and his father, Jack, worked one job at Gates Rubber his entire life. Jack lost his own father when he was three years old and dropped out of school after the eighth grade to get a job that helped his mother raise him and his brother. Jack joined the Navy when he was 17 after Pearl Harbor, and his brother, Bill, was killed in 1942 aboard the USS Yorktown during the battle of the Coral Sea.

"Dad was very involved with us in the church, and we went camping all the time, but sports just weren't where his interest was. My parents loved for us to participate in sports but they almost never came and watched. It didn't affect me and I didn't dwell on it. I just went on and did what I did. I knew they cared and they loved me," said Mains. "Before that last game I made a point of asking my parents to come watch me play.

"Lutheran came out in a box-and-one and I barely touched the ball in the first quarter. I didn't start shooting until I figured out how to rid of the guy guarding me. I just went further out and shot from out there.

"It was like everything I threw up went in and it was really fun. The guys on the team were having fun with it too. We played the same game we always did, but I was just in that zone. Maybe it was because my parents were there."

Jeff wound up with 42 points. It's still the school scoring record at Denver Christian. That was before the three-point rule and many of his shots were from three-point distance.

Regular season results can be misleading, but the team and I believed we were the best class AA team in Colorado that year. Midway through the season, we went up to play Broomfield. They were the top-ranked team in AA, and we beat them 69-61. Jeff had 25 points and Eldon had 11.

Two months later, Broomfield beat Yuma 54-47 to win the AA state championship.

After I announced my retirement, I received an e-mail from Dave Taylor, a starting guard for that Broomfield team:

"The game (when Christian beat Broomfield) wasn't actually an eight-point game. It should have been more like 15," Taylor wrote.

"That game was a turning point for us. It toughened us up both mentally and physically and probably helped us win the state championship. I knew and so did a few of my starting teammates that there was a better team in 2A that year and after we defeated Yuma to win it all, I said a silent 'Thank you' prayer that Denver Christian wasn't allowed to play in the tournament. I don't think there was any way we could have beaten your team if we had played you again in that 1967 state tournament. You know, you have really won nine state championships if '67 had counted. I clearly remember watching you along the sidelines that January day in Broomfield, a day that definitely influenced my life at several levels."

It's always rewarding when your players come back to see you, and Jeff and I had a chance to bring our relationship full circle.

"It must have been 30 years or so after I graduated, but I finally got the chance to tell Dick what he meant to me," said Mains. "I told him that the two men in my life that really impacted me were my father and him. He was the one who really challenged me in my faith, in my personal life, in my relations with others on and off the court. He was the one I looked up to as an example. I wanted to be successful like him.

"I would come in early and leave late. I could see his competitive fire. He got me going on the direction I wanted to go."

Jeff and his family spent many years in Albuquerque where he was a businessman and a very successful soccer coach at Hope Christian. He came back to Denver in 1999 and joined our staff as freshman coach (his grandson, Jeffrey was on the team) in time to be part of the final championship.

"He welcomed me with open arms. I was very hesitant, but we would finish a freshman game and Dick would always tell me to come sit beside him on the bench for the varsity game," said Mains.

We had successful teams in several sports besides basketball, but we didn't have any official district or state trophies in our case. I knew that had to change if we were going to take our athletic programs to the next level.

CHSAA's attitude toward admitting private schools seemed to be that they didn't want to mess with us. They were happy with the status quo of strictly public schools which, to be fair, was the norm across most of the country in the 1960s. When Ray Ball became the commissioner in 1966, some of us in the private school ranks sensed an opportunity.

Regis coach Guy Gibbs and Ray Ball were friends from officiating college football together. It didn't take long for Guy, St. Mary's football coach Eddie Kintz, and myself to begin meeting with Ball to talk about the private schools joining CHSAA.

CHSAA opened the door in 1966 and Regis and Denver Lutheran were the first private schools admitted.

The final barrier for Denver Christian's admission to CHSAA was the requirement that member schools field a football team. My dentist had a client who convinced us that Denver Christian needed to make the move. When the school administration committed to the sport, I looked around for a coach who had football experience. It didn't take a math major to solve that equation.

I was the only teacher in the school who had played the sport, so I became the football coach. It was the hardest job I have ever had. I spent a good share of our family vacation that summer in Lynden, WA at my in-laws' house writing a football playbook that we could use. That fall I met at 6:30 a.m. daily with the two colleagues who had agreed to be my assistants and taught them how we were going to conduct practice after school that day.

The first problem: we didn't have a field. We convinced the city of Denver to agree to a fee of $100 for the rights to develop a vacant field across the street from the school. Volunteers leveled the surface, laid sod, donated materials, and had it ready to play in time for the initial varsity season in 1969.

We only played a JV schedule in 1968, but that was enough for us to get into CHSAA. Our little school at the corner of Evans and Pearl could now compete officially in the highly competitive Metro League with a complete program and test ourselves against the state's best in post-season play.

The timing was especially good for the basketball program. Our last "independent" team finished 18-2, losing to Limon by two points on the road after beating them soundly at DC, and to Adams City. Two starters and seven other varsity players returned from the team and several other players had been toughened by the experience of that first football team, which finished with a 4-5 varsity record.

Starting the football program helped me realize that my coaching future was in basketball. I wasn't yet the kind of basketball coach I wanted to be, but I decided I was better able to coach basketball players than football players — even though I'd had a lot more success as a football player than I did as a basketball player. Too much time had passed between the last time I played football in 1953, the fall semester of my senior year, and 1970. I thought things had passed me by. I think I did a good job of teaching the football players the fundamentals and getting them ready to play a game and not get run over, but I wasn't very knowledgeable about the nuances of the game.

Football did have a significant carryover value to our basketball program. Both Ron Bosch and Tomm Vander Horst, who anchored our football line, transferred that physicalness to the hardwood. Playing football made them mentally as well as physically tough. They had a 'don't mess with us' attitude. They were both good rebounders and good inside players.

Defending state champion Brush with future college players Brendy Lee (who was drafted by the Atlanta Hawks after lettering three years at Nebraska) and Terry Christiansen had beaten us 59-41 in the season's fourth game at Denver Christian, but we went undefeated through our first official Metro League season. We won the state-qualifying tournament to get into the Final Eight of State the first year we were eligible.

The old Auditorium Arena downtown holds a special place in the hearts of all Colorado basketball fans of a certain age. Built in 1908 to host the Democratic National Convention, the Arena was home to national Amateur Athletic Union tournaments, the Denver Rockets (later Nuggets) of the American Basketball Association, and was a prime spot for high school games. It was also the first place Led Zeppelin played in

America—as an unbilled opening act for Spirit and Vanilla Fudge.

The Arena was intimate enough that the first row of fans sat very close to the floor. Opposing players would complain they were harassed and occasionally grabbed by a few over-zealous Rockets fans.

High school championships regularly drew capacity crowds. I had spent some nights sitting in the upper deck watching the Rockets and their star Spencer Haywood, so I was thrilled to be coaching my team from courtside in the state tournament.

Since the middle of January, I thought we had the potential to go deep into the tournament. The biggest concern was how they would respond to their first taste of official state competition and needing to win three games in three nights to win the championship. What gave me confidence was the knowledge that all through our years as an independent we had always been competitive against the bigger schools we'd played.

I still get goose bumps today when I think of our first state tournament. The community and the team had great anticipation and excitement, and in our first game against Crowley County we showed some jitters. Once we settled down, we won quite convincingly 67-49.

The second night it was a real battle with a pesky Lake County who were runners-up the previous year. But we made free throws down the stretch for a 66-59 victory and a berth in the finals.

On Saturday night, March 14, 1970 in front of 6,400 fans, including my parents who came in from Sheboygan, we faced Brush for the chance to win our first official state title.

We played a 1-3-1 zone as our basic defense and stayed in front and back of Lee, who was 6'8" and could really hurt us inside. Our bottom guy was maybe five feet from the corner, and my memory is that Christiansen made a couple from the corner and made me think about the wisdom of my strategy, but I didn't want to be impulsive and change things.

Ron Bosch led us to a quick start, but we gave up 24 points in the second quarter and went into halftime tied 34-34. Bosch picked up his third foul, and I put us into a slowdown game to

1970 CLASS AA STATE BASKETBALL CHAMPIONS

Standing, L to R: L. Wimberly-manager, J. Nydam-trainer, R. Bosch, C. Shannon, J. Wykstra, G. Afman, T. Vander Horst, B. Van Heukelem, T. Afman, D. Zoetewey-manager, Coach Katte. Kneeling: T. Bliek, M. Anema, R. Kroonenberg, J. Zoetewey, R. Schemper

pull Brush out of its zone and eat up some clock until we could get Bosch back into the game.

The game was tied at 44-44 with just over six minutes left when we put up nine consecutive points. Lee fouled out with four minutes left after scoring 19 points, and Bosch finished with 27 as we pulled away to a 62-49 victory.

Winning that state championship in our first year in CHSAA put us on the map. When we got back to the Denver Christian gym that night, it was full of students and fans ready for a post-game celebration. Both Bosch and our 5'9' guard Mark Anema made the all-state team.

I just had to pinch myself. Up until that point I thought I was a man who'd been given the job at a basketball school and worked hard to keep the tradition going. I believed in myself as a coach, but I was also in a basketball community that always thought if we'd have been allowed to be in the state tournament, we'd have won it.

I was young, and it helped me believe in myself more by reaching that level, but I don't know if I put a lot of extra pressure on myself to win the next one. I was proud the basketball tradition at Denver Christian was being recognized.

At that time I became more driven, maybe lost a little of the perspective that the game is for the players. The glamour and whatever that goes along with a championship became too important for a while. Then I realized that winning the state championship wasn't what made a good coach. It was how I dealt with players and how I motivated them and "grew" them.

We got to the final eight in each of the next three years but couldn't get over the final hurdle. One of the losses stayed with me for a very long time and left me with a painful but necessary career lesson.

In the 1972 tournament I believe I cost our team the championship. We were ahead of Eaton by 12 or 13 points after three quarters and I told them to slow it down, pull Eaton out of their zone and make them guard us. Well, we never could get going again, and we lost by a point.

It was hard for me and a couple of the players to not blame ourselves. As I said to those players, 'I get more chances but you don't.' After over 40 years, some still carry that disappointment with them, and I feel bad that we didn't win it. It's one of the lessons for life from basketball: about how you deal with adversity.

The impression it made on me—and it's stuck with me the rest of my career—is 'don't stop doing what got you there. Don't watch somebody else and think we should be doing that.'

Chapter 4: Bloom Where You are Planted

As the victories and championships mounted, larger high schools and even a few colleges reached out with offers to perform on a bigger stage. One phrase resonated emphatically in my mind: "Bloom Where You Are Planted."

What that always meant to me was that I didn't have to change schools or "move up" the coaching ladder in order to receive fulfillment as a coach. Each person must have a mission and vision to become the person God gifted him to be.

"Bloom where you are planted" doesn't mean you should not be upwardly mobile in your career. It does mean that if you are happy where you are that you should carefully examine the opportunities to prosper both professionally and personally in that environment before you make a decision to move on.

That being said, there were a few times when the situations and glamour of the new opportunities enticed me. I was no less ambitious than the next man, and coaching is a wellspring of striving upward. So when others called I listened.

Several suburban schools with enrollment significantly greater than that of Denver Christian came calling. Kent Denver, which was created in 1974 by merging two elite private schools, had moved to a 225-acre campus — an athletic director's dream. I had serious conversations about joining them as athletic director and coach.

The closest I came to leaving DC was in 1981 when Trinity Christian College, a school affiliated with the Christian Reformed Church in Chicago's southwest suburbs, considered me for the job as head basketball coach. Ironically it was my love for math, not basketball dreams that kept me at Denver Christian. Neither Trinity, nor my alma mater, Calvin, who also showed interest in me back in 1968, would allow me to teach math because their coaching positions were tied into the physical education departments.

All of us who have coached at smaller schools know that the size of the school doesn't determine the level of coaching that takes place. Ken Shaw and Ron Vlasin, just to name two, have won Colorado state championships in small towns as well as at schools that compete in the state's largest classification.

I was confident I could be successful at a higher level, but I knew that it wouldn't necessarily make me happier. My happiness wasn't dependent on my status. I was more interested in making a difference in the lives of young people. I could do what God called me to do, and stay at Denver Christian.

Simply put, I felt at home there. My fellow teachers socialized together. I felt I was an integral part of the Christian community; school was a part of it and church was a part of it. I felt not only comfortable, but also challenged.

When I arrived at Denver Christian, I was welcomed into the coaching fraternity immediately. Veteran coaches such as Bill Weimar at George Washington HS, and Hugh Bradley at Alameda HS reached out to me as a young coach. They invited me to participate in their summer clinics and scheduled scrimmages against my teams.

One of the best things I ever did in terms of learning more about the game of basketball was to bond with my fellow coaches and become a member of the Colorado High School Coaches Association. Some of the veteran coaches were very welcoming to a young coach, and as I became known in the profession, I have always tried to return that favor whenever I got a chance. I was determined to "never forget where I came from" and always tried to be a resource for young coaches.

"What sticks out the most to me about Dick Katte is how he talked to people. Players, coaches, fans, staff — all people. You would never know this was a multi-championship coach. Very humble and very appreciative of his role with young men," said Rudy Martin, who won a boys championship at Columbine and now coaches the girls at Green Mountain.

I consider myself blest to have been able to be an influence at Denver Christian that extended well past the classroom and the basketball court. I became the athletic director, assistant principal, director of admissions and was able to serve as an ambassador for Denver Christian on several fronts, not just in sports. I bloomed where I was planted.

When Mark Swalley, who spent 17 years as Denver Christian's principal, was just out of college and trying to decide whether or not to accept a teaching position at Denver Christian, I took him for coffee after his interview. We wound up sitting together for 90 minutes.

"I walked out with an overwhelming sense that I had just left the presence of someone very special. You don't truly know Dick Katte unless you understand how important building community is to him," Swalley said at Katte's official retirement ceremony. "As an athletic director he occasionally had coaching meetings before the school day began, other times they met at his house. He and Lorraine often invited coaches and teachers to their home and arranged social gatherings around school events.

"He was first and foremost a teacher. His love of teaching and being around young people has given him his youthful presence and outlook on life. He would be the first to tell you that good teaching is as important as good coaching. It is his teaching on the court, in the classroom or at a social event that he becomes the stuff of legend.

"Whether it is with a young and impressionable coach or conducting just one more interview with the media where he never fails to talk about his faith, Dick has taught us all how you truly walk your talk. Denver Christian has long been the standard bearer for Christian schools and others in Colorado in large part because of what he has done. That's a priority list that, when consistently carried out over 52 years becomes legendary. His influence on Denver Christian continues to be a model of excellence and we will forever be grateful to have called him our Coach."

As my career progressed, I was able to become involved in state and national coaches' and administrative organizations. I was honored to serve as president of both the Colorado High

School Coaches Association (CHSCA) and the National High School Athletic Coaches Association (NHSACA). I was invited to Washington DC to confer with the Department of Justice about young people and drug issues. Those experiences allowed me to bring Denver Christian's mission and name to those levels and also to be exposed to fresh and innovative ideas to bring back to my school.

I served three terms on the Executive Committee of the Colorado High School Activities Association and remain active in CHSAA in my retirement.

"It's not an overstatement to say that without Dick Katte, Denver Christian would not have gotten into CHSAA when it did," said Commissioner Paul Angelico. "He came back here, created a football team and did whatever it took to become part of it, and the association is better because of having both public and private schools. Whenever the CHSAA board would come to a loggerhead it was inevitable that Dick would say, slowly, 'Well ... you know' and he'd usually come up with something that everybody could live with."

During my tenure with the NHSACA, I became involved with the Women Athletes' Voice of Encouragement (WAVE) program. Their major sponsor, Ocean Spray, funded grants, awards and college scholarships to female athletes in the mid-90s when girls' participation in sports was about half that of boys'.

The financial support from Ocean Spray helped bridge the participation gap between male and female athletes, and helped us all realize that an important part of high school athletics is to provide equal opportunity to both sexes. The courts, through Title IX, had picked it up, but this was a way of saying that we didn't have to have the courts to tell us what had to be done and bring about equality.

I certainly didn't need to move to a bigger school to gain publicity for my career. For most of my tenure, Denver was a vibrant and competitive newspaper town. At their peak, *The Denver Post* and *The Rocky Mountain News* had a combined circulation that approached a million copies each day. And Scott Stocker's *Colorado Sidelines* newspaper, a popular and influential weekly newspaper that gave voluminous coverage to Colorado's high school players and coaches. In those days the media gave us as much attention as the big schools. We were well known in the basketball world of Colorado, and I know there were young people who came to Denver Christian because they wanted to play for me.

"When I was starting Colorado Sidelines nobody knew who I was or what I was doing, but Dick was one of the people who treated me like I was an important part of the media. When other people saw that a coach of his stature was cooperating with Sidelines it opened a lot of doors. I'll always be grateful for that and for the way he conducted himself, win or lose," said Scott Stocker, longtime prep sports reporter and a member of the Colorado High School Activities Association Hall of Fame.

Both Denver daily newspapers devoted a substantial amount of coverage to high school sports in that era. I enjoyed my relationships with the media. It was fun to talk about the game and the players — a little less fun when we lost, of course — and I always believed that the writers enjoyed the high school atmosphere and coming to Denver Christian High School.

"I can't remember a more accommodating coach. It always amazed me that someone of his stature in the profession was one of the first guys who would return his preseason information sheet, meticulously filled out. He did right by his kids every single year. He was a true gentleman to cover. It didn't matter whether he won or lost, he was the same. What a testament to him being able to do it for so long given the washing machine cycle of high school sports that rinses you out pretty quickly because of the outside pressures," said Gerry Valerio, *Senior Writer/State Association Director at Max Preps and former high school sports editor at the* Rocky Mountain News.

Fact is the Dick Katte Athletic Center got a lot of attention on its own as one of the state's iconic pit/bandbox facilities when it was featured in 2012 along with three other gyms in *The Denver Post*, as one of the "old school treasures." And I think our players were surprised when they watched the movie Hoosiers to see how much our gym resembled the one in the fictional town of Hickory, Ind.

When the last regular season game was played there near the end of the 2013-14 season after it was announced that Denver Christian would be moving to a new suburban facility, Neil Devlin called it "a unique combination of pit and Americana, one of the glowing, timeless symbols of the neighborhood off South Pearl Street and Evans Avenue."

Of the new gym's namesake, Neil Devlin of The Denver Post *said "He's a symbol of what's good about high school sports. When you're around him you just want to smile. When you're in his presence you feel like you owe it to him. When I first met him I quickly realized that I could trust him and I valued that he would answer your questions, wouldn't beat around the bush. He understood that dealing with guys like me was free press for his program and a chance for young people to experience dealing with the media like the pros do."*

Getting our players exposure and having their names in the papers gave our players a better chance for post-season recognition, and the publicity helped reinforce the image of Denver Christian throughout the state.

For all the attention that is paid to what happens in the gymnasium on game nights, a high school teacher and coach has contact with many more students in the classroom than he does on the basketball court.

"I always loved math and learning from him," said Greg Ham, point guard on Katte's undefeated team. "When I went off to Colorado College I was sort of intimidated by a lot of kids from the east coast and prep schools, but in my first two calculus classes I got the highest score and I thought, 'Wow, he really did prepare me.'

"He was very methodical and enthusiastic about solving algebra equations. He'd be up at the board going through a problem, interacting with the students in the class, and showing real joy when someone got it. It was the same thing with basketball. He would bring the team in; build different offenses and techniques like boxing out. In math class he would build blocks upon blocks of math principles. I can see a real similarity between his approaches to teaching math and coaching basketball."

Another player, Don Schneider, was the star on my first team, and though I was proud of his skills on the court, I'm even more proud of his distinguished career as a teacher, coach and administrator in Jefferson County.

"You always had the feeling he was looking out for you, had his eye on you," said Schneider. "He was a mentor to me. He led me down the path of coaching and teaching math. I adopted a lot of his attitude about teaching; his presentation, his expectations of kids and getting to know them outside the classroom as well."

An advantage of being at a school like Denver Christian, especially back in the 1960s and 1970s when we were essentially a neighborhood school, is that you get to know your students both in and out of school.

Lorraine and I were going out one night, and we asked Don's girlfriend, Ilene, who is now his wife of 48 years, to babysit for us. The rule was that the babysitter was not allowed to have friends come over while we were gone. Don, being a teenage boy, figured that as long as he stayed on the porch and talked to Ilene through the screen door that no one would be the wiser.

Imagine Ilene's surprise when the first thing I said to her when we arrived home was, "What was Don Schneider doing over here?" It didn't take much detective work. I knew Don was always snacking on pistachio nuts and our front porch was littered with shells. I gave Don a hard time about it the next day at school but I have to admit it was pretty funny.

The assistance teachers and coaches give to their students usually comes from the head and/or the heart. Occasionally it comes from the wallet and I'm certainly not the first teacher who has reached into his or her own pocket to aid a young person.

Troy VandenBroeke was a three-sport athlete who came back to Denver Christian and eventually became our head football coach. After he decided to give up high school baseball and switch to track, he sold his catcher's glove to another student for $60. He put the money in his locker before basketball practice and at the conclusion of practice it was gone!

It was a double blow to me. In addition to feeling sorry that Troy had lost his money, I had to deal with knowing that someone had violated the sanctity of our locker room.

"That was a lot of money for me," recalled VandenBroeke "My family made a lot of sacrifices so I could go to school at Denver Christian. To this day I don't know how Coach Katte found out about it but the next day in school he came up to me in hallway and handed me $60. He said, 'I know this happened and I'd like to give this to you.' To me that captures everything about him."

I also told him, "I hope you learned that when you're out in life that you need to lock your house."

Then there was Mike Hartman, one of my players whose girlfriend now wife, Stephanie, was a manager for our team. He said I told him that when you couldn't hang on to the ball, the best thing to do is to find a pretty girl to squeeze your hand. I don't remember saying that, but now that I think about it, it makes pretty good sense. The entwined fingers were a pleasant way to strengthen his grip.

Even though I knew my coaching focus was going to be with basketball, football would always stay close to my heart. After coaching football for four years at Denver Christian, I began to officiate football, first at the high school level then in the Western Athletic Conference.

It was a good way to stay in shape and it let me be part of a sport I loved on a regional and national scale. And once again it was proof that I could be involved in sports on a higher level without leaving the place where I felt so at home. I could bloom there too.

For all the success I've had on the scoreboard, the thing I'm most proud of is the way our teams have demonstrated sportsmanship and respect for our opponents. It was nurtured not only from my own Christian faith, but by my long affiliation with the Metro League and the deep friendships that developed among coaches and administrators which allowed me to emphasize Denver Christian's relationships with other schools.

There was a night when some of my players stormed off the court without congratulating archrival Holy Family after they'd handed us a difficult loss. I delivered a very stern lecture in the locker room about sportsmanship that those players remember to this day — and they reminded me of it during a get-together after my retirement.

"His legacy is an incredible story that one man could stay at one school and be so well respected for so many years and continue an awesome program and a culture of winning. Honestly, the culture that he created wasn't about winning, it was about raising young Christian kids to go out in the world and be successful. He was able to stay from generation to generation, continuing his program by making changes regardless of what decade it was. That's difficult to do for a lot of people," said Bruce Dick, who coaches at Resurrection Christian and won a state championship at Green Mountain.

In May, 2005 I returned to the place where I had found education, direction and my partner in life, to receive the Calvin College Distinguished Alumni Award. As I was preparing my speech for the awards luncheon I had a chance to reflect on my life's milestones and setbacks (including two life-threatening medical challenges) and the lessons they have imparted:

This is how I concluded:

"God gives us but one life to live, and a purpose to live for. Through these transformations in my life, God has enabled me to bloom where I was planted, and this truly speaks of the faithfulness and love of God."

The next day I participated in Calvin's commencement ceremony where I shared the stage with the day's graduation speaker: President George W. Bush.

Turns out it was President Bush's second visit to Calvin. When he was governor of Texas in 2000 he was part of a nationally televised debate among Republican Presidential candidates moderated by the late Tim Russert.

During his commencement speech, the President issued a call to service to the graduates that certainly resonated with me:

"It is your choice to make. As your generation takes its place in the world, all of you must make this decision: Will you be a spectator, or a citizen? To make a difference in this world, you must be involved. By serving a higher calling here or abroad,

you'll make your lives richer and build a more hopeful future for our world."

Of all the things I remember from that day, one of the fondest recollections is after President Bush finished his speech, he shook hands with everyone on the stage as he was leaving.

I said, "Thank you for coming. God bless you."

He looked me in the eye and said, "He already has."

When it was my turn to address the graduates I told them, "I know none of you are going to remember my name; you're just going to remember me as the guy who spoke after President Bush." I thought that was pretty good company for a boy from Sheboygan who grew up to accomplish all that at a small Christian high school at the corner of Pearl and Evans in Denver.

What I came to appreciate during this journey was that it is not the size of the stage that matters nearly as much as the richness of the role. My commitment to young people could be realized in my present setting. As I took a close look around me, it was apparent that I had the perfect situation: relationships with young people, respect in the community, good colleagues with whom I enjoyed working and a loving and very supportive family.

I valued those interactions with students, colleagues and family and became convinced that the rewards at Denver Christian probably couldn't be surpassed. I could do everything God called me to do without leaving Denver Christian. So long as I was committed to those ideals of service to my students, my school, my church, and my family, I could bloom where I was planted. And I leave that as a challenge to everyone.

Dick Katte greets President George W. Bush at Calvin College on May 21, 2005. The President delivered the commencement address, and Katte was honored as a Distinguished Alumni and also addressed the graduates, telling them "You're only going to remember me as the guy who followed the President." (Credit: Steve Vriesman)

Chapter 5: The Headache That Almost Killed Me

I almost never had a headache. The flu was going around in early December 1984, and some of its victims reported bad headaches. But nothing like the one that hit me when I was headed for my second-period class that day. I grabbed the rail to steady myself and was light-headed, dizzy and had double vision. I felt as if my head was about to split wide open.

I was 48 years old, healthy and in good shape. Besides spending more than two hours a day on my feet during basketball practice, I had just completed my first season as a Division I football official, and I spent my Saturday afternoons running up and down Western Athletic Conference fields.

This was Tuesday of a game week. We would meet Machebeuf on Friday, then University High School on Saturday. Our team, not highly regarded in preseason speculation, had opened with a victory over Mapleton, and a glimpse of hope was visible over the horizon. I didn't have time for this headache nonsense.

I got through my second period class, barely, but when I went to chapel the next hour, the pain started in the back of my neck and came roaring up through my head. I taught the rest of my classes but came home right after school.

Lorraine, who worked as a pediatric nurse at Porter Hospital, tried to convince me to take a sick day on Wednesday, but I refused, establishing a pattern of denial that would continue throughout the week. I finally let her make a doctor's appointment for me — so long as it coincided with my free period at school.

We were relieved at the diagnosis, an inner ear infection, but neither one of us was fully convinced that explained the way I was feeling. I still felt lousy, but we thought the antibiotics would knock it out in a couple of days. The doctor placed no restrictions on me, so I was on the bench as we lost to Machebeuf on Friday night. I remember the band sounding extra loud that night, and while I was grateful for the enthusiasm they generated, it made the pain in my head a lot worse.

The Saturday bus to Greeley for the game against University at Butler Hancock Hall on the University of Northern Colorado campus was leaving at 4 p.m. As I left the house, I told Lorraine, "I might be back." She and our daughter Laurie were worried because I had never missed a game and wondered what was going on.

I was sitting in my office just off the hallway at Denver Christian a few minutes before the bus was to leave when my assistant Ray Van Heukelem poked his head inside the door.

I could tell by the look on his face he knew something was wrong, and I told him, "You and Keith (my son and our freshman coach) are going to have to coach the game tonight. I can't go!"

Ray told me later he felt like time had stopped. He asked me what was wrong, and I told him I had a headache so bad I couldn't stand it.

I went home with a fever and chills and fell asleep immediately. Ray made a successful varsity-coaching debut, and we won 67-59.

By Monday, whatever it was that was raging inside my head had grown exponentially worse. Among the symptoms was a pain behind my eyes. A follow-up doctor's appointment and x-rays yielded another mis-diagnosis: acute sinusitis. Again, not great but we thought a new round of antibiotics would get it under control. One of my first thoughts was that I probably wouldn't have to miss another game.

Then the roof caved in. By late afternoon my condition deteriorated rapidly. I threw up violently, lost consciousness, came to and said "Oh God" in one of the rare times I invoked the Lord's name outside the context of prayer. Before long, we were in the emergency room at Porter's. The initial diagnosis was meningitis or encephalitis but after I had a CAT scan, the results were far more ominous.

The neurologist told Lorraine that there was bleeding in my brain, and we needed a neurosurgeon immediately. There was one in Denver, Dr. Gary Vander Ark, who I knew well and is an expert in the field. Lorraine asked the neurologist to call him.

Dr. Vander Ark and I have been friends since we were students at Calvin. He played basketball there, and I had spent a lot of time around the team and their coaches. I had been impressed at how much the players on the team seemed to like each other and how that translated into success. It was an observation that would be reinforced throughout my career.

He had wanted to be a brain surgeon since he was in the third grade. He earned his MD in neurosurgery at Michigan and moved to Colorado in 1970. He and his wife, Phyllis, went to the same church that we went to, and their son, Tom, played basketball for me at Denver Christian. Dr. Vander Ark was chief neurosurgeon at Swedish Hospital and the physician other doctors sought to treat their most difficult cases.

He transferred me from Porter Hospital Emergency to the ICU at Swedish Hospital. He told me "This is *very serious,* Dick," when I told him I didn't want to go because I had so much to do the next day. An arteriogram revealed the bleeding in my brain was an aneurysm: a blister, a weak spot about the size of a pencil eraser, in a blood vessel. I'd almost certainly had it since birth.

"It was right in the middle of the brain, between the two hemispheres, right on top of the optic nerves going to each eye. It's one of the more difficult places to have an aneurysm and can only be corrected by surgery," Vander Ark explained. "It is the most dangerous surgery you can have."

He called my entire family together and laid it out for them: 33 percent of the patients who have a brain aneurysm don't make it to the hospital, 10 percent don't survive the surgery and 20 percent who survive undergo personality changes. My condition was critical, and my family knew how hard they would have to pray for me and for Dr. Vander Ark.

His wife was afraid an operation like this would be too stressful for him to perform on a friend of 20 years. That made sense, but he knew he was the right man for the job.

"No other neurosurgeon had as much experience as I did at doing this. I did not feel in good conscience that I could have anyone else do it," recalled Vander Ark, who had written several papers about the surgical treatment of this particular aneurysm.

He was the son of a minister and he took spiritual guidance from the Book of Esther, specifically chapter 4, verse 14, that deals with a person placed "in this position for a time such as this."

"I couldn't ignore my responsibility even though I didn't want to operate on a friend," said Vander Ark, who served as Director of CU's Neurosurgery Residence Programs and founded the nationally acclaimed Doctors Care program, which provides more than $15 million in volunteer care to underserved populations in the south Metro Denver area. He also summited Mount Rainier in 1995.

These days, roughly half of aneurysms like mine are treated endovascularly, through a catheter that fills the aneurysm and isolates it from circulation, but in those days everyone had open surgery.

It was cold and snowy on December 13, nine days after that headache had knocked me for a loop on the staircase. Our pastor, Reverend James Kok, prayed with the family, and although I have no memory of it, asked me if I was ready to meet the Lord just before they wheeled me away on a gurney. While I was in surgery, Reverend Kok prayed and read the Bible with my family, focusing especially on Nahum 1:7: "The Lord is good, a refuge in times of trouble. He cares for those who trust in him." He offered comfort to the family while I was in surgery.

Dr. Vander Ark told us that the surgery was dangerous if everything went well but was potentially catastrophic if things didn't go well.

Things did not go well!

The biggest difficulty of operating on a blood vessel's blister that has recently hemorrhaged is that a little clot forms to stop the bleeding and this relatively fresh clot can give way during surgery, triggering major bleeding.

That's exactly what happened to me.

About an hour into surgery, while Dr. Vander Ark was in the process of retracting the brain so he could see where the aneurysm was located, the clot popped.

"It was like trying to deal with a garden hose that's on full blast," Vander Ark recalled. "We're operating down through a little tunnel and the point where the hemorrhage occurred is at the end of the tunnel. It's very difficult to evacuate the blood fast enough to see what you're doing. We have a couple of suckers that have to enter the field and we have to put a little spring-loaded metal clip across the base of the aneurysm. My prayers were answered and the clip turned out to be in a perfect location. We got the aneurysm without restricting blood flow to the brain."

More than four hours after I entered the operating room, Dr, Vander Ark met with Lorraine and the children and told them the surgery was successful. He even joked that he had taken out a piece of my brain, but he stressed that the next several days would be critical.

"Patients remain in danger for the first week or so because when there is a hemorrhage, the blood on the surface of the vessels causes the vessels to respond by going into spasms and the vessel's normal response is to clamp down. There's a risk that it would lead to a stroke," said Vander Ark.

My family was advised that the location of my aneurysm made me susceptible to changes in personality and judgment. Boy, did they ever.

When Dr. Vander Ark walked into my room in the Intensive Care Unit the next day, I greeted him by saying, "It's the Great Swami from the East." It was probably the last thing he ever expected to hear out of my mouth and it told him that my brain had suffered some 'insults' from the post-operative spasms.

The after-effects turned me into a less-than-ideal patient. I'd built my basketball program on being disciplined but my brain was sending different signals at the moment. My family tells me what a difficult patient I was for several days, and I have absolutely no memory of my time in the hospital.

But I learned that many family members and friends all over the country were praying for me during that time. The Lord wasn't finished with me yet, and I still had a lot of work to do. One of Lorraine's favorite Bible passages during this time was Ephesians 3:20: "Now unto him who is able to do immeasurably more than all we ask or imagine..." And He did more than we could imagine — as He granted me healing and a "second life."

Nine days after my surgery, Dr. Vander Ark received a telephone call from a nurse at Swedish Hospital.

"She said, 'I don't mean to alarm you but we can't find yor patient, Dick Katte. He's not in his room. Security is looking for him'," recalled Vander Ark, with a chuckle.

"I went down to the hospital and to my surprise he was back in his room. I said, 'Where did you go?' and he said he had to go for a walk outside to the corner store to get something."

I had just been transferred from the ICU unit to the ninth floor. After my wife left, I found the elevator and walked out of the hospital in my robe and slippers to the store. It felt good to be outside in the middle of winter but my judgment certainly wasn't good.

There were some touch-and-go days ahead, and I got a few stern lectures from my friend, Dr. Vander Ark. He told me that it would be a long recovery. On Christmas Eve morning, he called Lorraine and asked if she thought she could handle me at home. She was anxious to get me back home but I know she was wondering if I would be OK after what I had been through. I was discharged that morning. My family had a very hard time convincing me that I had been in the hospital for two weeks and that I had been seriously ill since I still had no memory of those days.

It was very confusing to me then, and as I look back now, I realize it was a miracle that I was given the great gift of a "second life" from God. Gifted doctors and nurses, the latest medical treatment and many prayers all played a role in bringing me back to health.

It was still step-by-step and day-by-day, but I returned to school after Christmas vacation with orders to teach only one class. I couldn't resist—I taught a full load even though I had an all-day substitute. Like I said, I was hardly the perfect patient. Lorraine asked me what the substitute teacher did all day, and I said, "She just sat there." Lorraine just shook her head. I was extremely tired when I got home those first few days.

Physically, my recovery was on schedule, but by mid-January, our family still felt I wasn't my old self. They felt like I missed basketball even more than I was letting on.

A week later I went to our game at Elizabeth High School. They let me sit on the bench, but I couldn't coach. We lost pretty badly, and afterwards some people commented about how tired I looked. Not quite seven weeks after the surgery I sat down with Dr. Vander Ark and asked if I could return to coaching.

"This was the worst team he'd ever had and my advice to him was the team's not going anywhere and this would be a wonderful opportunity for you to recover and let somebody else coach. He wanted no part of that. By that point in time it didn't make any difference in terms of putting his body at risk. I said if I were you I wouldn't do it but if you really want to, you can," recalled Vander Ark.

I was back on the practice floor that afternoon, and four days later I coached my first game since the surgery. We lost 48-33 to our rival, Holy Family. They gave me a nice welcome before the game, and Channel 9 showed up to do a story about my return.

Returning to the bench was the right medicine for me, even though we lost four of our last six games and were blown out 82-54 by Lutheran to wind up with a 6-14 record. I am convinced that getting back to coaching was the impetus that brought my brain back to the person I had been. I remember how good it felt...and how tired I was.

God had stepped in in a very dramatic way to remind me that He was in charge. Lorraine said the aneurysm changed me. She said I wasn't as driven as I had been and took more time to appreciate what was around me, to smell the roses.

As usual, she was exactly right.

The following year when we became "empty nesters" she became even closer to me—she became the coach's coach!

Chapter 6: The Making of a Coach — Over Time

When someone has coached for as long as I have, every one wants to know about the changes in the game or the changes in players over those years.

Changes in the game are evident, from the much looser interpretation of "palming" the ball to the enormous impact of the three-point basket.

Players too have changed. Physically they are bigger, quicker and more talented, and the culture has created a completely different lifestyle.

The biggest change — and it has affected coaches and administrators in all sports — has been the parents. It used to be about the team and players. Now it's about MY son.

There is no longer the respect and trust that came automatically from "Coach said" because today the players have too many coaches.

Now it's "Coach said, but I don't agree." When I grew up, the coach was revered and that probably wasn't always healthy, but the coaches were the experts of the game.

The parents and the players felt that the coach was the one who knew the game. For the first 15 years I coached, nobody ever said, "Why?' I'm trying to remember the first time a player came to me and said, "Well, my dad (or mom) said ..."

I don't think anything good results if your players or their parents question the coach and the way he does things. They have to believe in you and your program, and know that you are not doing things flippantly or without good reason. They must trust the fact that you are the coach, and that your decisions are well thought out and are good for the team. It's nice to have that trust which is the result of commitment and loyalty to you as a coach.

Coaches have always had to deal with parents and outside interests such as summer league coaches, but those pressures have never been greater than they are today. So many parents believe their players are Division I prospects, and that you as a coach have a duty to "showcase" their talents. One coach who used a 10-player rotation to win a state championship came under fire from some the parents for not giving their sons enough of a chance to build up gaudy statistics.

My approach to allowing parents to attend practice is probably different than many other coaches. When I started at Denver Christian we relied on parents to do a lot of things for us, and they were very cooperative and supportive. Some of the dads had played for me, and I never reached the point where I felt they shouldn't be there. If they attended practices they needed to follow my rules: Stay in the bleachers away from the coaches and players and have no contact with your son via comments or "coaching."

With all the media attention on individuals — when was the last time you saw a four-pass/no dribble fast break leading to a layup featured on ESPN's Top 10 Plays of the Day? — it's more important than ever that players know and accept their roles. One of the most important things a coach has to do is make players understand what they need to do for the team to be successful. It's easy to convince a player that he has to score for the team to win. It's not so easy to convince his teammate that he has to rebound and defend and sacrifice his offense so that teammates can take more shots.

The individual player has to buy into his role and carry it out. It's easier if you are winning because everyone wants to contribute to success, but if parents are always talking to their sons about their box score, players become the victim of hearing two different things. The coach will say to a player, "You did a great job on the boards tonight," but when he gets out in the hallway, some parents will say, "Why didn't you take more shots and score more points?"

As a coach, you have to highlight the contributions each player is making, especially the ones who are not big scorers and know their roles. It's not often that you get a player like Riley Herren, the point guard on my last team, who only cared about getting assists and rarely took more than two or three shots a game. In fact, several of our games that year were one-sided, and I occasionally put Riley back in during the fourth quarter if he hadn't scored yet. I virtually had to order him to try and score just so he would get into the box score in the newspapers.

When we had our first undefeated team our leading scorer was a sophomore, Craig Matthies. I'm not sure the other four starte rs — all seniors — were crazy about that at first, but they could appreciate his role as a scorer.

We have been fortunate at Denver Christian to escape many of these problems. Partly it is due to the success our program had and the credibility that it brought to me and to my coaching staff. It was also advantageous that many of our players had fathers, brothers and uncles who had come through the program before them. This helped them understand the culture and they wanted their sons to be a part of it.

I know fellow coaches at both public and private schools who spend far too much time dealing with outside distractions caused by overzealous parents. I think this situation has driven some outstanding young coaches out of our profession, and that is a profoundly sad development.

Coaches need to have the support of their athletic director and principal as long as they are obeying the rules, treating players fairly and with with respect and conducting themselves in a manner that reflects integrity. No coach should have to make decisions about playing time or who makes the team through the filter of "Is this going to come back and haunt me because of what the parents say?"

Understand that I am not making the case that a coach should not be held accountable for his actions. I am saying that those actions need to be respected as the decisions of a professional who has the best interests of each player and the entire team at heart.

As long as I have coached, I don't think it's ever easy when the players or their parents question me, and the way I do things. As long as I know that I'm not doing things flippantly or without good reason, and that my decisions are well thought out, I am at peace — but it's nice to have trust.

I grew up in an era where the prototypical coach was authoritarian and operated from the principle that his players would improve if he instilled fear in them by degrading them and trying to belittle them. I was determined to establish the fact that as coach I could help a person more if I was reasonable and caring. If I can exhibit those qualities, I believe players will try hard to live up to my expectations. I've had parents say "He'll run through a wall for you," and I think that's about as good a compliment that a coach can receive.

Years ago there were times when I walked into my house after a game, and the phone was ringing. It was a parent calling to question and berate me. It was then that I established the rule that a parent cannot talk to me for 18 hours following a game. Neither one of us is in the right frame of mind to hear what the other one has to say immediately after the game. There is too much emotion and not enough rational thinking right after a game.

When I realized that my role was not to be my players' friend but to mentor them and teach them, I became what the coach should be — someone they respected and trusted. I am to be their coach, their teacher and their role model. It may have taken a few years, but I think I developed that rapport with my players. Even when I had young assistants I insisted that they maintain their distance. If the coach is the players' friend he will have a hard time dealing with issues or disciplining them for improper behavior.

I've always tried to develop players who were good teammates. If they become a group of good teammates it will be a memorable experience because everyone wants everyone else to do well, and the team becomes like a "family." That doesn't just happen nor is it always possible just by saying it at your first team meeting. It is something that is caught rather than taught. When it happens, your team will be good regardless of their record. Team unity and togetherness can only happen if each player realizes and believes that success is determined by the degree of teamwork and TRUST.

The style of your offense can also enhance teamwork. When we started playing Air Academy High School, Bob Spears was

Two smiles tell the whole story as Katte holds the trophy after the 2005 championship. (Photo by Jan Forseth, ImagesoftheWild.com, copyright 2005)

the Air Force Academy's head coach, and his son was a star on the high school team. They were running the shuffle, which definitely fosters passing and team play. Everyone handles the ball. Everyone shoots the ball. There isn't that syndrome that the ball has to go to one player. When we played Air Academy we couldn't stop them, and I always assumed it was because they ran the shuffle so well. (The shuffle offense got everyone involved, so I added it to our offensive playbook.)

Every young coach wants to do things his own way, but he should also want to study what good coaches do. I'm going to guess that there was seldom a year when I didn't go to at least one coaching clinic and take home at least one or more useable items. The zone offense we call "Kansas" came from a clinic presentation by Walter Shublom, the coach at Wyandotte High School in Kansas City, Kansas. He had one of the most successful programs in the country. He won 10 Kansas state championships and as a young coach I was very impressed with his attention to detail and teamwork.

I learned a lot of things from Al Harden, the coach at the University of Denver in the 1970s. I was sure his sons were going to come to Denver Christian, but he went back home to Indiana and his boys became stars back there. Irv Brown was instrumental in motivating and convincing me to start a basketball fundamentals camp in Southeast Denver. We kicked off Katte's Kamp in 1973 and taught the fundamentals of basketball to youngsters from fourth to eighth grades, and ran it successfully until 2009.

I was the National Basketball Chairman for the National High School Athletic Coaches Association in the late '80's. The NHSCA sponsored clinics around the country and I rubbed elbows and exchanged ideas with Dale Brown, who was LSU's head coach for 25 years, and Dean Smith, who led North Carolina for 36 years to great success. One of the people who made a big impression on me was the late Jim Valvano, whose North Carolina State team won the 1983 NCAA championship, and then died of cancer 10 years later. I liked what he had to say and the way he related to people.

The person who hired me at Denver Christian was Ray Lucht, who had played at Nebraska. He was the math teacher, then became the principal and later was the superintendent.

He didn't have a very strict or demanding style because his players were so in tune with him. That old phrase about KISS (Keep It Simple, Stupid) was what he did, and he definitely impacted me.

People like Hugh Bradley at Alameda made me feel included in the Colorado coaching fraternity. It was because of Hugh's recommendation when Green Mountain High School opened in 1973 that they hired my first star player, Don Schneider, as a teacher and coach.

Don was one of the people who influenced my opinion that freshmen shouldn't play on the varsity. When younger players play with the older players they are placed in a new culture. When they are playing on the varsity and their classmates catch up to them, socially they don't know their teammates very well, because they always played with older players. Also, sometimes they seem to plateau in their later years.

I always wanted my assistant coaches to be coaches, not just assistants, and anybody that ever sat beside me on the bench often thanked me for allowing them to give input. They always knew they had the right to speak up. I didn't want them to think that I had been around so long that I didn't want their advice. I feel really good about these relationships, and in my 48 years I never had to release an assistant. My philosophy for assistants was that they had to believe in what we do, be loyal and have a good rapport with the players. They must be committed to teaching the fundamentals and basics. The only things I demanded from my JV coaches were that they always play man-to-man defense and try to get everyone in the game. I never said how much they had to play any given player, and I never said they couldn't teach zone, but I wanted their players to know how to play man-to-man defense when they got to the varsity.

When I started at Denver Christian in 1960 Ray Van Heukelem was in the seventh grade. I was his JV coach and then his varsity coach. He taught and coached in Florida after college, but returned to Denver in 1974 as the ninth grade coach and then took over the JV team. By 2006 he had been my assistant for 32 years, and I think he thought, "This guy is never going to die or retire." So he went to Littleton High School as the varsity basketball coach. After we won the back-to-back state titles in 2005 and 2006 would have been a great time to go out, but I just didn't feel like I was ready to leave the game.

Ray and I had a great comfort zone together. I listened to him more than anyone except my wife. He brought new and creative ideas to me and to the game. He was always comfortable suggesting and critiquing what we were doing, saying, "Why don't we try this?" I'd say, "First, let's see how it works for the JV team." He designed the press breaker we were still using when I retired.

It seemed only fair that Ray was hired as my replacement when I retired. I was very proud that he won the state tournament in his first year as varsity coach with only one starter back from our team the year before.

It is hard for a coach who's looking ahead, looking down the bench and trying to keep abreast of what's happening on the floor to keep the statistical part of the game in his mind. I must confess that, as a math person, I always knew the point difference but seldom knew which player was doing the scoring. I would know who's hot and who's not, but I was more interested in how WE were playing and who was contributing to our success.

I know there are times in a game when a player should come out and other times when he must stay in. If the player is leading the team with his passing, scoring and hustle and is not hurting the defense, he should stay in the game unless the score dictates otherwise.

We know even star players need a rest, but sometimes momentum or the score doesn't allow it. Seldom would I know how many points or rebounds a player has.

I can remember keeping a player from breaking our school scoring record, and I was not aware of it.

Grant Mudd was a three-year varsity player and a very good one. In his junior year (1990) we were leading the league late in the season but were being challenged by rival Kent Denver. The game was back and forth and every time Kent Denver scored, we answered — mostly by Mudd. A three-pointer and a couple of free throws by Grant widened the margin, and with two minutes left, I thought it would be good to let Grant get his applause for his great game.

He received a standing ovation from the crowd and a hug from me. Five minutes later in the locker room I was informed that Grant had scored 41 points when I took him out of the game — one point short of the Denver Christian scoring record of 42 points. I apologized to him. I felt bad I had taken him out, but he understood. He went on to play baseball at the University of Denver and is still my friend today!

I can't over-emphasize the impact math had on my coaching philosophy. I carried the logic and sequential nature of math into the way I organized a practice. I believe that if anyone analyzed the degrees and background of basketball coaches, math would be the second most prominent discipline behind physical education because of the sequential nature that leads to success in both math and basketball. I love it when I have a team where the whole is greater than the sum of its parts. I know in math it's equal, but in good basketball it's greater than. Whenever the team under-achieves, the whole is less than the sum of its parts.

There are not many coaches who play five-on-five as little as I did. I spent a lot of time playing three-on-three as the basic set, and then progressed to four-on-four and, finally to five-on-five situations. In fact, if I were inventing the game of basketball from scratch, I would probably make it a three-on-three game. There are three-on-three tournaments across the country today, and they are very popular.

I always made sure I informed my players where they stood and what I expected from them. When we finished that last camp or tournament in the summer I wrote each one of them a letter saying, "Here's what our team accomplished. Here's your place on this team. Please work on these specific things so that when we next come together in November you are a more complete player and can fill the role given you."

Having a good relationship with the officials was important to me, but it didn't start out that way. When I was young I was a bit more volatile and tended to blame officials occasionally. When I became a football official, all that changed completely. That's when I realized that I was spending too much time complaining and not doing what I was paid to do and that was to coach. A coach should never say that an official cost him the game. We have to understand that the officials are part of the game, and just like me and my team, they're not perfect.

"One thing I always remember about Coach Katte is if you made a foul and looked over at him like 'That was a terrible call,' he'd say, 'Yes, you did foul him' loud enough for the officials to hear. He would never let you blame the officials. His message was, "If they're going to call that, stop doing it.' When I started officiating, some coaches would complain about everything, and the players take on the personality of the coach. You hear them complaining instead of focusing on the game. On the rare occasion that Coach Katte would say something, you figure he's probably right. Being a football official he had a lot of respect for basketball officials," said Kent Hamstra, a veteran basketball official who played on DC's third championship team and whose son, Andrew, also played for the Crusaders.

I seldom got a technical foul — maybe six or seven in 1,109 varsity games. It's not that I didn't ever disagree with an official's call, but I didn't ruin my credibility by harping on every single call. If an official doesn't hear me complaining the whole game and then I do speak up — and do it tactfully — I am more likely to get his attention. He is never going to reverse that call, but he might take a closer look at the next call.

When a coach only picks up a handful of technical fouls in his career, people tend to remember them. Ray has shared the story of my first technical in my very first game when I jumped up and shouted "Oh no" when he was called out-of-bounds in front of our bench.

Probably the most demonstrative technical I ever earned—and there's no doubt I earned this one — was against Clear Creek in the early 1990s. Skip Bennett, then the coach at Clear Creek, went on to be an assistant at Western State College. He told the story in a video at my retirement celebration:

"Dick and I probably played each other 60 times and I won twice. During a game at our place in the early '90s, probably the worst block-charge call in the history of basketball went our way. I looked down to see what Dick was going to do.

"He stood up like he never stands up, walked out of his coaching box and I thought 'Uh, oh.' Then he's at the scorer's table right next to me, then he's in our box, then he's chasing this referee all the way down to our wrestling room. The referee says, 'Coach I have to give you a technical.' On the way back Dick says to me, 'That was fun, that was worth it!'"

I both respect and appreciate officials. I can call many of them my friends. We wouldn't have a game without them, and the vast majority of them take their jobs very seriously. I always believed in treating them like I wanted to be treated: with respect and professionalism.

I took my role as the face of Denver Christian boys' basketball very seriously and never wanted to do anything to tarnish it. As I look back, I'm certain that had an effect on my demeanor on the bench. Besides, with dozens of whistles being blown in a typical game, how many of them are going to have a direct bearing on the outcome of the game? I can get my point across to the officials without being rude and overbearing.

At my retirement celebration, Bob Wood, against whom my teams had some epic battles while he was winning two state championships at Buena Vista (he is now the coach at Mountain Vista), called me a "master manipulator of officials." Since they used to say the same thing about John Wooden, I'll take that as a compliment.

Lyle Weiss, a respected official who has worked many state tournament games, said that whenever he heard me say, "Holy cow" or "suitcase" (when I thought an opponent had traveled), he knew they'd probably missed a call.

After 10 years of high school football officiating I was fortunate enough to be hired to work Western Athletic Conference games.

I remember when I was working a Fresno State game, and their coach was notoriously loud. In the third quarter he was

Katte making a three-pronged point in the huddle. (Photo by Alan Hart)

complaining to me on the sideline about something that happened in the first quarter. I finally said, "Coach, your players were playing very well when you were coaching, but they haven't played very well since you started officiating."

Being a football official not only gave me a greater appreciation for basketball officials, but it also forced me to concentrate on football in the fall and not be obsessed with basketball. It also greatly strengthened my understanding of the coach/official relationship.

My greatest strength as an official was the rapport I could establish with the guys on the sideline. In 1998 I retired from officiating, and during my last season, I worked the Rocky Mountain Showdown — the Colorado Buffalos/Colorado State Rams game — in old Mile High Stadium before a crowd of 76,000. The noise from the crowd was incredible, and the day was filled with excitement. My final game that year was Northwestern at Hawaii when Gary Barnett was the Northwestern coach. That wasn't a bad road trip to finish with!

Teachers have to remember how much students are aware of your mannerisms. There's always the class clown who loves to imitate you, and I have to admit some of them can do it pretty well. When I was teaching math I always rolled the chalk back and forth in my hand. I don't know if it was part of my thought process or just a habit, but it definitely became part of the image of Coach Katte and anyone who was trying to perfect their imitation of me had to have that as part of their act.

I scouted quite a bit early in my career. I always liked to see a team once before we played them and more than one time if they beat us. When we became empty nesters, Lorraine often went along with me. She kept a shot chart, and after a half when we had seen their tendencies, we left. I realized I didn't have to see the opponent so much, but that the best way to play an opponent is to do what we do better than they do what they do.

One thing I wish I would have realized when I first started coaching is that the essence of the game is not a new offense or a new defense. Instead, it's getting players to believe in the fundamentals and what we are doing and that being a good teammate is much more important than the offenses and defenses we would teach them.

Over-coaching is one of the biggest hurdles a young coach has to overcome, especially when his team advances into the tournament. They were good enough to get there doing what they did all season. I don't think it's necessary to add all these special things just because they are in the state tournament. For the team's morale, it's good to give them something new to think about. I believe I always put in something new for state, but I'm not sure we ever used much of it.

I think one becomes a good coach when he realizes he has done his best, and there are some things he just doesn't have control over. If he has done everything necessary, he must realize some things are out of his control. "Play hard, do your best, be a good teammate and leave the rest to God." These have been my words to young men and coaches for many years. I know I became a better coach when I learned this.

Coaching is almost always a pleasure — except on the day you have to tell a student there is no place for him on the basketball team. Usually I would do it the day after tryouts were finished. I wanted to sit down with my assistants and evaluate the prospects. When the decision was made I looked for a chance to get the student in my office so it was as private as possible. In all the years I had to cut players, I always talked to the player personally rather than just posting a list of names of those who were on the team.

The player is probably going to hang his head a little. I have to tell him I know how he's feeling. I tell him I've made an objective decision and that if there's any way to find a place for him in the program, I will. Somewhere along the line, successful coaches have built up enough trust and respect that it might hurt the student for a while, but down the way he will understand. I have cut some players who then came back the next year and turned out to be good teammates. I want to use that person as an example of a player who really wanted it, and worked hard to get a second chance.

When it comes to choosing captains, the players are pretty good. They know who they want to lead them, and it's not always the star player. In the last eight years alone, I had three cases where the best player wasn't the right person to be a captain. That's nothing against the star players — they just were not comfortable or capable of taking that leadership role. I have used co-captains most of my career; I believe it's good that they have each other's opinion, and the respect issue works better.

The coach has to exert his right to choose the right leaders. I would never overrule someone who was chosen by a vote of the team, but I reserved the right to add another captain if I felt we needed someone stronger in that role than the person the players chose or someone who cared enough to confront.

There was a time when I would choose captains during the summer, but I think that got to be too demanding for some players. In the last 10-15 years we have held tryouts, chosen the team, had about a week of practices and then had the players elect the captains. Then I would meet with the captains, ask them what our strengths were, what we needed to work on and what they would do as the team leaders.

I always chose one of those elected captains as a game captain and then added one or two others to go to midcourt to get that exposure and the chance to be a leader. Standing at center court before a game, being a representative of your school and shaking hands with the officials and the captains from the other team is something I don't think players ever forget.

Practices are for coaches, games are for players — I don't like that, but it's realistic. And game days are special.

The most important thing on the day of a game is having a routine and a timetable. Some things you can be flexible about, others you can't.

The players like to dress alike on game days. It can be anything from khakis and a collared shirt to jeans and a dress shirt and a tie. Whatever they decide — and most of the times I let the captains choose — they're all going to dress alike. It's important for teams that they remember who they're representing. The student body can identify the players as a team on game days. When we play at home, I will be more lenient but a team like Limon never is. I've never seen a team of theirs come off their bus without a tie. They have taught their players it's an expectation — even if they have to ride 90 miles on a bus to their game. It may be uncomfortable, but to the team it's important.

My players were required to be in the gym five minutes before the start of the preceding game, whether it was our JV team or we're playing a boy/girl doubleheader. I expected them to sit together before the team — not with their girlfriends.

I filled out the scorebook, but I didn't fill in the starters until I saw that all my players were on time. If it was a road game, I set a time when the bus will leave and if a player was not there, the bus left without him.

We warmed up during halftime of the JV game — just enough to get the kinks out with layups, passing and partner shooting. It also helped them begin their focus.

With approximately two minutes left in the third quarter of the JV game, my team went to the locker room. That was their time. They had a devotional by themselves — remember, I taught at a Christian school and this won't be applicable for everyone. I wanted them to talk to each other a little bit about life and about the game.

I liked to have the players come and get me when they were ready. There were some things I needed to put in their hands. I wanted them to be able to make good decisions, and they knew when they are ready to hear from me. With about six minutes to go in the JV game, they'd send up somebody to say, 'Coach, we're ready.' The bigger the game, the longer it was before they come and get me. That means they'd taken care of their business, and I didn't have to worry about how much time I had to talk to them.

My pregame, halftime and postgame talks became more conversational as my career progressed. I'd talk about us first and what we're going to do. I'd give them a few keys (take care of the ball, stop whoever and whatever was needed for that particular game). Then I'd talk about the other team, who was going to defend who and what we needed to do against them. "We've practiced all week, now here are your assignments." I'd remind them to know whom they were guarding when they enter the game. Maybe I'd use 30 seconds for a little motivation, ask them if any of them have something to add and sometimes one of the players will say something a little energizing.

As we hit the floor, there were many times that all the momentum created in the locker room was lost because the preliminary game was not over, so we'd wait and fidget. As a result we seldom BURST onto the floor. As a result, I learned over the years not to get them sky high in the locker room but to build that momentum through spirited warm-ups and talking.

As I stepped on the floor, I'd get a feeling of being settled. The anxiousness and uncertainties (the 'what ifs' or 'then whats') were gone — I was in the place I had been waiting to be (all day, all week), and it gave me a good feeling. Before the game coaches are often asked "Are you nervous" or "What do you think?" My standard answer was "If I don't have a feeling of excitement, then I should no longer coach."

Usually the first thing I did was survey the surroundings to see if everything is as it should be. I looked to see where Lorraine (and my family) are seated and how active the crowd was. Then I would settle in and observe the opposing team's warm-ups, make mental notes and double check the scorebook. Having done my routine, I usually went over and visited with my opposing coach. After all that, I awaited the start of the game, often comparing thoughts with my assistant coaches. I got focused.

I can't over-emphasize the importance of warm-ups. It has to be structured almost like a mini-practice, but can't become purposeless. I believe my players must do things that get them ready for each part of the game. I want to have some drill with defense because that's what we stressed so much and also wanted to have something with passing.

We progressed from passing, layups and then shooting. After they've done their shooting, we use a 3-on-2 drill, and finish with the shell drill for a couple of minutes. Get them used to talking. We want them to break a sweat in the warm-ups because to start the second half, they have to break a sweat again. Too many teams aren't ready to start the second half because they didn't warm up properly. I always tried to get our team onto the floor with at least three minutes left in halftime. My last words in the locker room were almost always, "Remember how important the first five possessions of the second half are." That's where games can get away from you so warm up hard.

Larry Bird was the epitome of preparation. I wish there was a DVD of his pre-game preparation. His shooting would always start close to the basket and then slowly move out, always maintaining exactly the same form. Not all players use their warm-up time properly.

I grew up in the era of the crewcut and coached through every conceivable hairstyle fashion. I admit it wasn't easy in the 70s when hair started getting long, but my players always had about the same kind of haircuts even if it was a little longer than I might have preferred. Two things were important to me: that your hair not be so long that it impairs your game because you're always brushing it out of your eyes and that you don't wear your hair in a way that distinguishes you from anybody else on the team. We don't call attention to ourselves — we are a TEAM.

One of the hardest things to get across to players is the concept of mental toughness. I have tried to create situations in practice that demand it, but some players are going to thrive on it and others are going to wilt. When I was a younger coach, I used to make light of it by saying, "You should sign up for the band or choir and be forced to play or sing a solo. You have to get up there and do it — it's OK if you mess it up once. You want the person who is willing to fail. The next time he will do it better." It's my job to get them there, and it's their job to deliver.

I've never liked fund-raising. When the team does fund-raisers, the coach creates obligations. It is as if he owes the player and his family something because they raised money for the program. I've resisted it as an athletic director and a coach. Without fund-raising, there are some things that we are going to have to do without, and that's a choice a coach has to make.

It's important for the coach to find people who are responsible to fill the support positions such as manager, filming and stats crew. I turned to my grandson, Carter, to film our games when he was a fifth grader. Like a lot of young people his age, he is very technologically sound. He is very loyal and took the job seriously. When I put his name in the game program, he was elated. It gave him status and sent the message that what he was doing was important to our program.

When I started coaching, every coach in my school was also a teacher, and I believe that's the best situation. Today, there are more and more people who coach but don't teach in the school. When people retire from coaching but stay on as teachers, it can be very difficult for a principal to bring in a person who can coach and also fits into a certain teaching position with a solid educational philosophy. It's definitely better if coaches are also in the classroom.

Many life lessons come from athletics, and I believe coaches miss something when they don't see the players in all the different settings of the school day. If one of my players is having trouble in a class I can go with him, sit down with the teacher and find out the issues, and how the student can be helped. I feel very strongly that it is to the student's advantage.

If a coach from outside the building comes in, he has to invest in the players for more than the time he sees them at practice and in games.

Dave Logan was one of the great high school athletes in Colorado history when he played at Wheat Ridge in the 1970s, and he went on to play nine years in the National Football League. Since retiring from playing sports, he has had a tremendous career in broadcasting as a talk show host and the play-by-play voice of the Denver Broncos, as well as great success as a high school football coach. When he took the Cherry Creek football job in 2012, he went to at least 10 of their baseball games as well as basketball and lacrosse games. He spent time getting to know teachers and administrators because he wanted the students and the community to know they were important to him, and he wasn't just about winning football games.

That's an excellent example of a coach who doesn't teach at the school going the extra mile to establish himself as part of the school's culture. Any non-teaching coach who doesn't spend time at the school outside of practice and games runs a big risk of being viewed as an outsider who isn't interested in anything else except his own team, their success and his program. All non-teacher coaches should work on this.

This chapter is a smorgasbord of coaching procedures and situations. Some of the items may be duplicates of items referred to in other settings. But I know they are really important if I mentioned them more than once.

Chapter 7: Culture, Faith and Trademarks

If you have a successful program with a strong tradition there are times when you may not have great talent, but your program and its tradition will give you good results when you might not have expected it. Such tradition is established not only by championships and victories, but also by philosophy, culture and faith.

These are the building blocks that I believe are the foundation for what we have been able to accomplish in the Denver Christian basketball program. Denver Christian is a Christian school, and some of the faith-based elements of our philosophy will not be relevant to a public school situation. However I believe the fundamental concepts of our program apply to any coach who wants to build a program characterized by these qualities and trademarks.

I don't think we can say that some sports are Christian and others are not, but I do know that basketball had its origins with a man who was known as a Christian. So it's rewarding that I have spent my life in a sport which is closely aligned with my Christian faith.

Did you know Dr. James Naismith, who invented basketball was a Christian? He was a devout Christian (an orphan who never finished high school) and rooted in the Springfield, Massachusetts YMCA.

His biography is part of basketball lore. He chose physical education over becoming a minister and wound up at the Young Men's Christian Association's International Training School for Christian Workers, the forerunner of what is today Springfield College.

Searching for a game that could be played indoors during the harsh Massachusetts winters in 1892, Naismith devised what he called "Basket ball" using a soccer ball and the iconic peach baskets.

Because of Naismith's religious faith and his support of the muscular Christianity movement (which espoused sharing faith through athletics), some have made the connection that basketball is Christian based and/or was intended as an instrument to spread the faith.

Michael Zogry, associate professor of religious studies and director of the Indigenous Studies program at the University of Kansas who is researching a book on religion and basketball, believes the connection is more nuanced.

"I don't think there is an identifiable Christian element to basketball, but I think Naismith thought about the values of teamwork, controlling your emotions and proper behavior that people might not associate with a specific religion," he said. "He believed basketball could serve as an instrument to achieve those goals. Less well known is that his game also was meant to help build Christian character and to indicate certain values of the muscular Christian movement."

Naismith's own words, in a speech delivered to the National Collegiate Athletic Association in 1914 and reprinted in the American Physical Education Review, indicate his commitment to sportsmanship:

"So much stress is laid to-day on the winning of games that practically all else is lost sight of, and the fine elements of manliness and true sportsmanship are accorded a secondary place. One great problem for this organization is the formulating of a system of scoring that will take cognizance of these traits to manhood or the development of traditions which will make it impossible for a college man to take advantage of an opponent, save in those qualities which the sport is supposed to require. The bane of basket ball to-day is the attempt to evade the laws of the game and even the rulings of the officials. There is no more reason why we should take an illegal advantage of an opponent in basket ball than that we should put our hand in his pocket and take his wealth. Few college men would take money or valuables from another, yet they are taught by the practices of our sports that it is not dishonorable to take an illegal advantage of another, if there is little prospect of being caught."

The inventor of basketball considered himself a teacher more than a coach and even refereed many of the games in which his teams played while he served as the first basketball coach at the University of Kansas. He invented a great game, and his legacy is a timeless commitment to the way the game should be played.

It is important that all members of the Crusader's basketball program understand fully the philosophy of the coaching staff. Underlying all education at Denver Christian is Jesus Christ. He is our Lord and all learning and playing is centered around Him, in the classroom and on the basketball court. ALL that we do must be to His glory! The spirit of Christianity must always be present individually and as a team, both in winning and in losing, in word and deed, in all aspects of life.

"In everything you do put God first..." —Proverbs 3:6

I strongly believe that, if our basketball program accomplishes nothing else than the development of character, it has been successful! Character is hard to measure but is always tested. Character is what you are in your heart; that quality that makes you what you are. Some examples of good character are citizenship, sportsmanship, dependability, honesty, respect, courage, reaction to emotional situations, leadership and the ability to live with others.

With that quality foremost in mind, I want the foundation of our program to have some basic ingredients, things that I call Crusader trademarks. This becomes our culture, the qualities that I want everyone to see every time they watch a Denver Christian team play. I have an overriding belief in the team approach to basketball: the game is for the players — all of them.

As coaches, we can get caught up in the idea that the game revolves around us and our success, won-lost records and championships. We can fixate on how hard we work, and the time we spend on designing practices, scouting, developing game plans and all the rest, but it is about the players. Basketball is for the players, and they should receive the benefits. They are out there on the floor: sweating, working hard, achieving various degrees of success, trying to make their dreams come true and sacrificing for the greater good of the team. We are grateful that many young men have blossomed with this emphasis and have left the program with a sense of importance and success.

Here are the basic characteristics that I worked hard to instill in our team, things I call "Crusader Trademarks."

SPORTSMANSHIP

Sportsmanship — which is the most important of our Crusader Trademarks — means "winning with class, losing in style, always being positive, and going the extra mile." Good sportsmanship is the Golden Rule applied to sports—it is the Christian way of participating. Our state governing body, the Colorado high School Activities Association, says it's "How you play the game."

How do we handle adversity and discouragement? What is our reaction when there is a bad call or a tough loss? I know that body language and attitude speak loudly in times like this. Sportsmanship is the impression that the public receives and takes away from the game. The score is soon forgotten, but the conduct and attitude remains forever in the minds of those who were most affected.

I would say that winning and losing should be de-emphasized because sportsmanship is more lasting than championships. Sportsmanship is winning, even when you lose the game. Every coach must realize that his role is paramount in this. I would like to be remembered as the coach whose teams were well schooled in the fundamentals and team play, were competitive, and showed courtesy, character and integrity. As coaches we must realize that we are in influential positions. We are role models and we must care enough to confront unacceptable behavior. I believe we must always remain composed and rational even when things do not go our way, and be fair in our analysis of officials and opponents.

Sportsmanship is a journey, which must permeate our character and our lives.

DEFENSE

Quite simply, defense is the heart of what we are. Championships are won with defense. Defense is hustle, footwork, position, and determination. Mental toughness is crucial in becoming a good defensive player. I believe ball pressure is essential, and each player must be able to control his man and know his teammates will help. The necessary ingredients are aggressiveness (diving for loose balls, getting your hand in the passing lane, beating your opponent to the ball), pride (the feeling that you can contain your man and force him into mistakes) and communication (the glue that unites five players into a strong defensive team). Getting stops is an important statistic for my teams. Later in the book there is an entire chapter dedicated to our defensive focus.

FUNDAMENTALS

The mastery of fundamentals is key to success in basketball and in life. I want all my players to execute the basics quickly and properly. These fundamentals should be learned early in the player's career so they can be blended into good team play. Bad techniques are hard to correct, so the repetition of fundamentals is necessary to form good habits.

INTENSITY

Always play hard (even when coach isn't watching.) There are no shortcuts to success. Hard work, hustle, and competitive spirit are characteristics. Momentum is always shifting. When behind, don't give up; when ahead, don't let up.

COMMITMENT

I want our team to be the most dedicated and determined team in the state. The players must be loyal to their teammates, their coaches, and their school. We must learn that hard work is the price that is paid for success and that we are able to work harder than we think.

UNSELFISHNESS

This ingredient will create great teams – be a good teammate, both on and off the court. Share the basketball, make the extra pass, encourage your teammates and recognize the good play of others. Be the person that everyone likes to play and be with. There is no I in TEAM.

SACRIFICE

The great teams are ones that give up things. I don't believe you can do everything else AND play basketball. They must make changes in their lifestyle for the well being of the team. They give up playing time or give up the ball for team success. **TEAM** to them must mean: "Together Everyone Accomplishes More."

These are the trademarks I want my team to personify. They are the basis of my philosophy of basketball, which has been shaped through 48 years as a head coach. In short we start with these.

A young coach beginning his first job or a coach that is asked to start a new program needs to establish a plan of action which will become the foundation — the culture — of that program. That plan must embody his personality and philosophy. Discipline and perseverance by staff and players will result in a solid beginning for your program.

In 1968 I was assigned the responsibility to start a football program from scratch at Denver Christian as a requirement for gaining entrance into CHSAA. To say we were unprepared would be a grand understatement! No one on the staff had ever coached football, and only two of the coaches had ever played football. We met for many hours answering such questions as

1. Where do we start?

2. How do we measure accomplishment?

3. How do we establish a timetable to reach a competitive level?

Our decision was to begin with fundamentals and conditioning and then establish our culture — the trademarks of the program. The first year was spent with players learning about every aspect of the game and playing at the sub-varsity level. By the second year they were competitive at the varsity level.

I believe the same approach and list of questions would be beneficial for anyone starting a new business, or for a young pastor called to plant a church.

Among the more troubling and disappointing trends I have witnessed in my career is the increasing tendency for young athletes to choose to specialize in one sport at a very early age (often in middle school or even younger).

I know that some basketball coaches encourage their players to devote themselves solely to their sport. I believe that is a mistake for both the players and those basketball programs and schools. Parents hear from coaches that if they don't specialize and engage in year-around training in a single sport (often at significant cost to the parents), that their child's chances of gaining a college scholarship are diminished but the fact is that the numbers simply don't bear that out. Athletic scholarships are difficult to obtain.

We established a tradition in our culture of encouraging multiple-sport athletes because it provides a healthy benefit for all involved. It promotes cooperation and communication within the athletic department, and it prevents the overuse and stress injuries associated with specialization. Successful programs must have an active off-season program, especially in the summer, but I have always bent over backwards to accommodate players who want to participate in another sport.

Colorado multi-sport athlete Dave Logan and I wanted to hold a town meeting through CHSAA about the value of being a three-sport athlete but were never able to arrange it. Troy Tulowitzki is a better shortstop today because he was a point guard in basketball. I think you develop toughness from playing football, hand-eye coordination from baseball and tennis, endurance from cross-country and track and patience from golf, all of which make a better basketball player.

There is great value to everyone involved when the good athletes contribute to the betterment of the total school program rather than just their specialty. I think athletes and their families become more loyal and have more fun, and the students improve themselves as persons and athletes.

I think an athlete should be a young man and a player, not just a player. I think they should know about fishing and other things that young men should learn about.

When I coached the All-State games in Alamosa the summer after my last season, Austin LeFebre was one of my players. He stayed in town the next day and went fishing with his dad. Something about that made me happy.

Chapter 8: Defense — The Heart of the Game

It takes more skill to play offense, but it takes more heart to play defense. I think that's why I've always had a soft spot for players who gave it their all on the defensive end, especially ones who might not have all the talent you'd like to see in a player but who made up for it with determination and hustle.

First you teach them footwork, the stance and the slides — they have to understand that we always expect to see this. Defense is just blue-collar work. When my program became known for its defense, it just sort of kept itself going. My players knew because their dads, brothers or teammates had told them "Coach Katte will like you if you play defense." There were very few years when teams averaged more than 50 points against us.

That's how Riley Herren, the point guard on my last team, got into the starting lineup. Another player was ineligible, so I put Riley in the starting lineup because he could stop the other team's star. He stayed there the rest of the season. Ron Kroonenberg, the point guard on our 1970 team, was also a great defender. I could tell him to guard someone, and we didn't have to worry about that player hurting us offensively that night. For a coach it's a great advantage to have a "stopper."

One of the ways to get players to play defense with their feet is to take away their hands. Sometimes I give them a towel and have them hold it behind their back as they slide in basketball stance; the towel occupies their hands.

If they don't move their feet they are going to get beat and when they can't use their hands, they learn quickly that hands are secondary to playing good defense. It is good to have active hands and use them to make the passing lanes harder to penetrate and get deflections, but if you don't play defense with your feet you're going to reach, grab, pick up fouls and get beat from the dribble.

Some of the points I have strongly emphasized over the years at Denver Christian are:

- Defend your opponent by using your legs.

- Force your opponent to receive the ball outside the foul line extended.

- Force the dribbler to move laterally from side to side, never vertically toward the basket.

- Keep your arm in front of the intended receiver and you will discourage him or intercept passes; get your hand in the passing lane.

- If your man gets by you on a dribble, get into the lane and pick up the free man.

- Force the man you are defending to use his weakness.

- Every shot must be contested. If the shooter has space to shoot, you haven't done the job as it should be done. Learn your spacing.

- Play off your man and in "help" position when the ball is on the other side of the floor.

- Stop the ball from going to the opponents' big man, especially at the foul line.

- Know where the ball and your man are on defense. Don't follow him – lead him.

- On baseline screens, never let your man go on the baseline side.

We do a lot of hedging whether we're playing man-to-man or zone. Hedging is when a player helps for half-a-count, and then has to get back to his basic position. I like it better than switching because it puts pressure on the man who's covering the ball to get back and cover his man. It's too easy to just call "switch" and let your teammate have to cover up for your weakness.

A player's stance tells me a lot about their commitment to defense. If they are flat-footed, they're either lazy or tired, and defense isn't a priority with them. This can't be tolerated. A coach has to bench players from the game if they're not in basketball position, and tell them that if they go back in, to use the defensive basics they have been taught. We start youngsters early on this. In our camps we get the players in a stance and tell them to see if they can get up and down the floor in that position—we call that basketball position. If the coach emphasizes it and rewards it, players will start taking pride in it.

The best team drill to teach defensive principles is the shell drill. We run shell or some variation of shell in almost every practice. The shell teaches jumping to the pass, fronting the cutter and help-side rotation, and it is a drill that all teams should use to gain defensive prowess. Once players get the basics down, we tell them they have to have three passes around the perimeter before they can try to score.

A defender should always step in the direction of the pass. I have stopped practice if the defender allows his man to cut through. It's an important quality that a coach has to emphasize if he wants to consider himself a good defensive coach. If the defender doesn't do it, his man is going to have an advantage. I've had teams and players who have done this better than others. It's great when there is one player on a team who believes everything you say, and you can use him to show the others what you're talking about.

The best thing I can do, as a defensive coach, is convince my players that good defense means the man being defended doesn't have the time or opportunity to look for his next option. He is so well defended that he can't do what he's coached to do. That means the defender has closed out well and has good ball pressure.

I know a lot of coaches have switched to the open stance in denying the ball, but I like the closed stance. I think it appears to the offense like a more aggressive stance. It's easier to get from a closed stance to an open stance than the other way around. If a player is going from open to closed he can lose his balance.

I believe in picking up ballhandlers just over half court in the backcourt. I want the other team's point guard to be forced to work hard to bring the ball up so that there might be no need to press anyone else. I want my team to be aggressive defensively and get out and pressure the ball. There may be some situations when it's OK to play "house" defense and have everyone inside the three-point line, but most of the time I want my players challenging everything the offense tries to do.

When you watch college games and the NBA on television you see a lot more coaches telling players to defend their opponents on the high side, to deny reversal and giving up some room on the baseline. But I believe that, especially in the high school game, only bad things happen when somebody gets to the baseline. If a player gives up the baseline, the other team doesn't have to reverse it and he has no help defense. I know if a team has good rotations and some tall players in the middle they can help effectively, but if I can convince my players that nobody drives us on the baseline we're going to be good defensively. If we have a player give up the baseline, we're going to stop practice and run for him. If I have a good offensive team, and we are allowed to get to the baseline, we're going to hit the jump shot or enter to the high post.

I think shot blocking is one of the worst things in basketball. Period. Most of the time possession isn't gained, and the defense lets down for a second. So many times when there is a blocked shot by the defense it winds up in an easy basket for the other team because they are behind the defenders and in better position to grab the loose ball. It's hard to teach players to stay down and to not leave their feet, but it's the sign of a well-coached team. Besides, it seems that about half the shot-block attempts wind up being a foul.

If there is anything we've failed at as basketball coaches, it's finding a good way to teach rebounding. Rebounding comes from the heart. I can teach players about how to pivot and to block out, but if somebody wants to get the ball more than his opponent, they're going to get it. I don't know that I ever took anybody who wasn't a good rebounder and turned them into a good rebounder because of the way I coached him. What's important is to show them a couple of principles — how to box out, keep their legs apart with good balance — but to emphasize that the most important part of rebounding is just going after the ball. We go through the boxing out drills: 1-on-1, 2-on-2 and 3-on-3, but the number one thing I've emphasized is we're not going to give them second shots. Players must be convinced that the ball has their name on it — they own it.

One of the weaknesses of zone defense is that nobody has a responsibility for a man in rebounding. If they crash with two guys against your low player, your player doesn't have any help keeping them away. With that being said, I think a smart player can steal a few offensive rebounds by getting to the baseline and then coming back inside the defense.

Defense becomes more important than ever when a team gets into the tournament. I don't ever remember having a team that played good offense all three nights in a row in a tournament, so the defense must come through. Many times teams will come out tight in the first game of a tournament. They are playing on an unfamiliar court, the backgrounds are different and it's natural to have trouble scoring. That's when the emphasis on defense is going to have to carry you. My last team couldn't make a shot against Sanford in the first half of the state quarterfinals but had only given up seven points by halftime. Defense like that will keep a team in any game.

When I started out as a JV coach, my thinking was that if I taught the fundamentals of man-to-man defense, then learning to play zone would be easily done. I have had a couple of career swings in my defensive thinking over the years. There were some years when I was more of a zone coach, but I still insisted man-to-man fundamentals be learned first.

One of the things about playing zone defense is that not a lot of teams have a good zone offense. Most teams try to attack it by shooting from the outside. In the '70s, zone was our primary defense. Even though the easiest ones to teach are the 2-3 and the 1-2-2, we played a flexible 1-3-1 (see chapter 9). The slides in that zone are so crucial and require a lot of anticipation. A team can cover a lot of weaknesses in a 2-3 and not get burned, but if that wing doesn't slide down in the 1-3-1, they are so vulnerable to the skip pass. In the 1980s and early 1990s we played mostly man-to-man with some 2-3 and then in the early 2000s we developed "a scramble" by extending the 2-3 with the guys up front having no rules — just hustle and create chaos.

The last ten years of my career, my teams were dominant man-to-man teams. The summer after we lost the state championship in 2002, I told our players, "We're going to learn how to stop teams." After that, man-to- man has been our bread and butter.

We didn't do a lot of trapping. I just wanted our guys to say, "You're my man and I can stop you." As a coach it's very important that the players learn to take pride in their defense. It's not easy because the fans and the media focus on who is scoring the points, but the coach has to emphasize how much he values the guys who are playing defense. There have been a few times when one of our players had a great defensive game but didn't score, and I've put him back in the game and told him to shoot so he could get into the box score. It's important for players to see their name as an important part of the team.

The first five minutes of a game are very important in setting the defensive tone. Officials want to get into the flow of the game, and they're looking to blow their whistle early on. Don't allow players to give them a chance to call a cheap foul in the first couple of minutes because that foul keeps them from being aggressive. Officials are like coaches. They see which team is committed to playing solid defense. I believe that as the game goes on they will give a player the benefit of the doubt on a close call if they've seen him hustle and play smart, intense defense all game.

In the early season we played a lot of man-to-man in practice. We'd make them get two stops in a row, then three stops in a row. We tried to have everything game-like and competitive and used a lot of breakdown drills to teach how to get stops on defense. My philosophy was not to accept excuses, but we have to be honest enough to say that none of us can stop a really good offensive player alone, no matter how good as a defender we are. I was demanding but realistic. Young people respond to reasonable expectations.

I've never been a coach who tried to make the players fit into my system. Coaches have to adjust their philosophy to the strength of their current team's players. One year, when we were bigger than usual, we could form a big triangle inside and play the 2-3 as our primary defense because it fit our personnel. It is even easier to hide a weak defender in a zone than it is with a man-to-man defense.

There are many ways to play a zone and teach the slides. Boyd (Tiny) Grant, who was the head coach at Colorado State and Fresno State, would send one of the players in the back of the triangle out to cover the wing and rotate his back line. College players are stronger and quicker than high school players, and I didn't think that would work for us so I always used hedging as my way of covering the wings.

When we played a lot of 1-3-1 I would sometimes have the point guard on top, and if they attacked it with two players I made the point guard cover both of them. Other times, if the point guard had good anticipation I put him in the back of the zone. If you have a point guard who is physical and can rebound a little, that's where I would play him because the bottom player isn't expected to get you a lot of rebounds. The rebounding responsibilities were given to the wings. Whenever I had a smaller player on the baseline I always had the wings crash the boards hard and outlet to the guard. I think we can ask too much of our zone responsibilities. Sometimes the more movement there is, the more players become confused. Just convince them that "nobody goes in my house."

It really concerns me to see elementary school teams playing zone defense. It is used all the time because youngsters at that age can't shoot from the outside, so the defense looks good but we hurt the kids' development because they are not learning the fundamentals of man-to-man defense.

I think a good team should be able to play two different kinds of zone and two different types of man-to-man. I also liked to have one good gimmick defense like a box-and-one or triangle and two. We would use it against a team with one (or two) great offensive players. It doesn't require a lot of preparation. If you know how to play a 2-3 zone, you just take one player out of the zone and drape him all over their best player. If we spent more than an hour and a half teaching that during the entire season that would be a lot. My math background gave me a good sequential way of presenting that to the players, and we used it successfully in several big games.

I would prefer to play the box-and-one in the second half or for only one quarter. It is also something that can be used when coming out of a timeout, and the players get excited about surprising the other team. Plus, it helps to work against a gimmick once in a while in practice, and then the players won't panic when an opponent springs it on them during a game. The key to attacking it, I believe, is not to run any special plays, but to start our best player at the post or at the point. Those are the hardest places to defend without creating gaps elsewhere and then run a regular offense against it.

I always emphasized defense more than offense in the summer so that when we began the regular season, our emphasis on defense was already a trademark. It was an accepted fact that we could play defense, so it let us get our offensive alignments and situations worked out in preseason. It's hard in the summer because we did not make it mandatory, and there are seldom the same players around for all of the summer games so it was hard to have an offensive flow. With limited practice time, it's more efficient if you stress defense during that practice time. So offensively that is one of the times when I let them play pass-and-cut, or wheel offense, and open up the floor without making it complicated. They could have fun on offense as long as they played hard on defense. Its counter to what most teams do, and when a team defends them hard in the summer a lot of these teams are confused. We really try hard to establish the roles of players during the summer play.

It is good to emphasize how important deflections are. If a player gets his hands on a lot of balls it disrupts what the opponent wants to do. It also convinces a player that he's into the game when he's getting deflections. He's aggressive and his deflection may have created something. How my players use their hands defensively is a product of how well I have taught them to use their feet. If they are using their feet effectively they're not using their hands to grab and reach, and they can keep them in the passing lanes. They don't have to steal the ball. If we are playing good defense many times the other team will turn the ball over to you.

Defending the flash cut is another important thing players have to learn. They must be there before their opponent is. If he is going to come across the lane and post up, get there ahead of him. Lead him—don't follow him.

A coach must to be willing to adjust to changes in the game. I was raised with the slide step for defensive movement, but I don't insist on it anymore. We've shown we can play defense as well or even better with the push step. It's much easier to do, so it would be foolish to spend so much time on a slide step when it is done better with a push step. Be consistent, but don't be rigid.

I believe the best way to guard a post player is to half-front him – put a hand in his ball side. If he is a real star, we might full front. For one thing, feeding the post has become a lost art. Teams don't practice the lob pass, and it's hard to do. If you have a post player with a big wingspan, sometimes it makes sense to have him play behind the other team's post as long as he doesn't think that's a license to try to block shots.

Defending the baseline out-of-bounds play is a very important situation because if done poorly it will result in giving up two or three easy baskets in a game and that can be enough to turn the game. At one point in my career, I was convinced that because there are so many good out-of-bounds plays its wise to play zone, so we played zone. Even when our 1-3-1 was good, we'd play a 2-3 to cover the corners. But in the last 15 years, because of all the good shooters and plays, my teams almost always played man-to-man. We use what we call "centerfielder" which means we don't cover the inbounder face-up. Our other four guys cover their man, and the "centerfielder" is covering all those cuts that bring opponents open to the basket. Many times we can get turnovers because they can't find the open man.

Our "centerfielder" starts in a position about three feet away from the inbounder but not with his back to him, because we've all seen the smart players who throw the ball off the defender's back. Once the ball comes in, the centerfielder finds his man. This may sound counter-intuitive but he's actually in a better position to cover him than if he was playing him straight up because he can react quicker to screens set for the in-bounder. And we don't have to switch big and little on inbounds plays.

We work on our transition defense when we work on transition offense. We teach our players to take two big steps toward half court, turn around and play defense. We teach them not to look back before they get to half-court because it will slow them down. They're better off getting back, then finding and reacting to the ball. I think it has been said that we don't need to do conditioning drills because everything we've done throughout practice has been conditioning in drill and transitions.

One more thing about transition defense: don't try to keep the rebounder from making the outlet. That leads to bad fouls because the player is reaching and grabbing in the open court right in front of an official. It's OK to let your player be kind of a deterrent to the rebounder so he can't throw it down the floor, but it's not worth the risk to be too aggressive.

I have seen many changes in the game over my career, but I never lost my belief that our emphasis on defense is non-negotiable. By that I mean that if a young man wants to play in our program, he must play defense. I can say that because if I can convince him that defense is our trademark, *any* player *can* learn to play defense. The adage says "offense wins games (and gets players recognition) but defense wins championships (and gives tradition to a program)," and we truly believed that.

Chapter 9:
The Flexible 1-3-1

I've always been proud that the teams I coached were recognized primarily for their defense. Although I have been always been a strong advocate of man-to-man defense throughout my career, I believe my team has to be able to play an effective zone. In fact, there were a number of years when we employed the 1-3-1 zone as our primary defense.

We chose the 1-3-1 as our standard zone because in normal position it covers the high percentage scoring areas well, and its weaknesses are in places where most high school teams have difficulty — the corners.

From the standard 1-3-1 we have developed our flexible defense, making adjustments as were necessary to cope with different offensive strengths, and to suit our personnel. Because this defense so easily incorporates the zone trap, we have used many of its principles in our defense.

When we began using the 1-3-1 for the first time we had ideal personnel for it, and we advanced to the state tournament in 1970 using it as our basic defense.

The basic alignment is in Diagram A.

Player X1 (Ron Kroonenberg) was our point man–the team quarterback. He was tough, quick and a tremendous hustler who, most of the time, covered the two players on the top if our opponents attacked us with a two-man offensive front. Player X2 (Mark Anema) was our other guard, a good defensive player and an excellent trap man. Player X3 (Ron Bosch), the other wing, was the best rebounder of our forwards, and could also push the ball up court after a rebound. Player X4 (Tomm VanderHorst) was a forward with good ball sense. Player X5 (Greg Afman) was our center who did an excellent job of keeping the ball out of the middle.

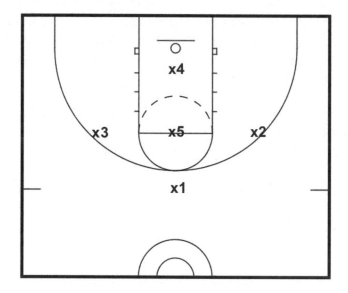

Figure A: Our alignment and personnel the first year we were full-fledged membes of the state association and thus eligible to play for the state championship (which we won). X1 is our point guard, a 5-10 player with the quickness and toughness to cover the two players at the top against a two-man offensive front. X2 was a guard with excellent instincts and skills to trap. X3, a 6-3 forward, was our best rebounder and someone who could grab a rebound and push it up the floor himself. X4 was a 6-3 forward with good ball sense and was a strong outlet passes but no someone we would want to push the ball himself. X5 was a 6-4 center who did an excellent job of keeping the ball out of the middle.

In our trap defense (Diagram B) we encourage the ball to go to the corners and then "open the gates," so that it looks as if the "whole student body" is coming at them. This creates an eagerness to get rid of the ball, and often resulted in a bad pass. Ideally we want the ball to go to X2's side of the floor to utilize his trapping ability and X3's rebounding strength, so we overplay our point man and X5 and bring X3 up in the zone. (Diagram B)

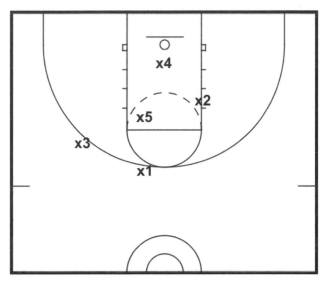

Figure B: We want to encourage the ball to go to the corner and then trap hard to try to create an eagerness to get rid of the ball, which often results in a bad pass. Because X2 was our best trapper and X 4 was our best rebounder, we overplayed our point guard (X1) and center (X5) and brought X3 up a little higher than he had started.

On the pass to the wing, our defense shifted as shown in Diagram C. Player X2 has coverage of the ball, X5 and X1 prevented the ball from going inside, X4 protected the baseline and X3 protected against the lob pass (like a free safety). When the ball reaches the corner we pressure it with the double-team trap and look for the interception (Diagram D).

One of the things I liked about the 1-3-1 was the flexibility it gave us to make adjustments for specific opponents either in our preparation or during a game.

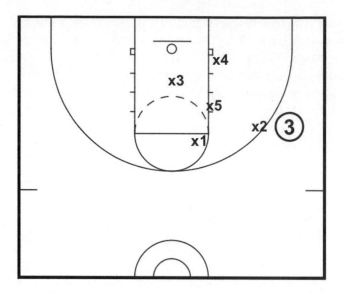

Figure C: On the pass to the wing, our defense has shifted with X2 having coverage of the ball, X5 and X1 preventing the ball from going inside, X4 protecting the baseline and X3 protecting against the lob.

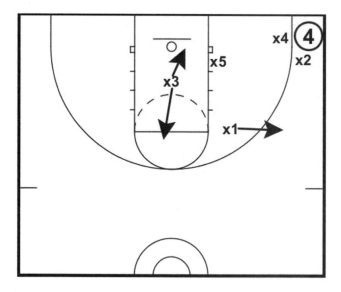

Figure D: When the ball reaches the corner, we pressure with a double-team trap of X4 and X2 instructed to keep their hands active and mirror the ball. Any tip or deflection of the pass will almost always result in an interception. If X1 strongly denies the closest reversal path to the wing, both X3 and X5 will be in position to make an interception/turnover.

After winning in the quarterfinals and semifinals using the 1-3-1, we advanced to the state championship game against Brush, who was the defending state champion, undefeated and riding a 34-game winning streak.

They had defeated us convincingly early in the season, and we made the decision to concentrate on the two players who had hurt us in that earlier game and force them to do things they didn't want to do. Because we did not want the ball passed into the post man—and because we didn't want the corners left open—we made these adjustments. (Diagram E)

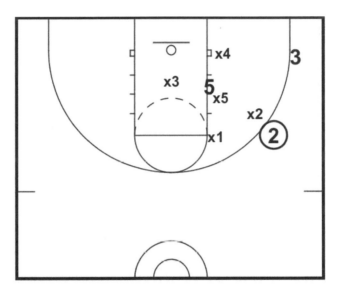

Figure E: In the state championship game we played a team that had been very effective against our flexible 1-3-1 when we played them earlier in the season. Our opponents had two future Division 1 players, one a strong post, the other a skilled wing. We had to make them do things they didn't want to do. When the ball went to the wing, X1 moved into the crease. X2 played slightly toward the corner. X5 fronted the post. X3 played behind the post and X4 edged slightly toward the corner.

With the ball at the wing: X1 moved into the crease, X2 played slightly toward the corner, X5 played in front of the post man, X3 behind the post man and X4 slightly toward the corner.

When the ball went to the corner, instead of our double-team as in our trap, we covered the corner with half a man—X2 was instructed to just get a hand in his face, and X4 was positioned 10 feet from the corner to encourage 3 to drive the baseline. When he did, X4 immediately covered him and X2 and X5 covered B (Diagram F).

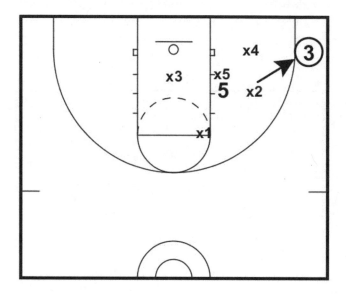

Figure F: When h ball went to the corner, instead of our usual double team, we covered the corner with half a defender. X2 was instructed to get a hand in his face and X4 was positioned about 10 feet from the corner to encourage the player with the ball to drive. When he did, X4 covered him and X2 and X5 covered the post. Their small forward did hit a couple of shots from the corner but we stayed with our strategy.

When the player in the corner didn't drive, X2 covered him with his left hand in his face, and X4 and X5 covered B. X1 and X3's responsibilities didn't change much when the ball was in the corner (Diagram G).

These were the adjustments we made in our flexible 1-3-1 zone. We also wanted to force 2 to go to his left if he did get the ball because we didn't think he was as strong going to his left. We walked through these assignments Saturday morning in our gym before the game, cleared up any questions and convinced ourselves it would work.

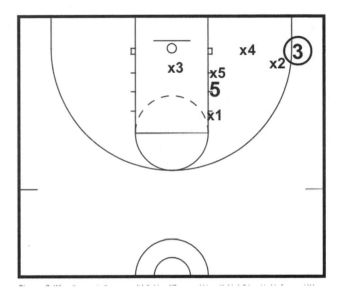

Figure G: When the man in the corner didn't drive, X2 covered him with his left hand in his face and X4 and X5 covered the post. X1 and X3 covered their areas to defend against passes. In the end, the strategy paid off and we prevailed 62-49.

The results were amazing. Only eight times were our opponents able to penetrate and get the ball to 2 (in diagram G) and on three of these times we forced him to go left and he missed badly. 3 was allowed only two shots from the corner, but he did score 19 points, mostly from around the perimeter. Although the game was tied at halftime and close throughout, we won 62-49 to become the 1970 state champions in our first year of official state competition.

Much of the material in this chapter is excerpted from an article Katte wrote for The Coaching Clinic Special Basketball Issue, *"Game Plans for State Championship Play" in October, 1970.*

Chapter 10: Everyone Likes to Play Offense

It doesn't take long to determine what part of the game players like best. Hand a youngster a basketball, and he looks for a hoop to shoot at. From driveways to school gyms to the nation's largest arenas, putting the ball in the basket is the first instinct of every player.

That's the reason why offense was one of the last sections covered in the handbook I gave to my players.

My philosophy was that defense and rebounding were the keys to a successful basketball program. If young men wanted to play at DC, they had to learn defensive fundamentals, intensity, and have the desire to rebound. A successful tradition was established with this emphasis, but the offensive skills of each team and player were not ignored; it's just that they weren't given the top priority.

Offense is like candy. You don't have to teach someone to like candy. Defense and rebounding? Those are the good-for-you veggies of the game.

Obviously, the main objective of any offense is to score; with an inside shot or an outside shot, with a lay-up or a jump shot, a two or a three. My belief is that this should be done in the easiest manner and as quickly as possible, and that the running game gives the best opportunities to accomplish this goal. The DC teams believed that they could fast break from any situation that occurs in a basketball game, from a rebound or turnover (steal) and after a basket.

When I first came to Denver Christian the team had eight seniors, and they were undefeated under Coach Ray Lucht, who was also the principal. They could push the ball and play together and that really influenced my philosophy. Another influence was Branch McCracken, who was at Indiana University while I was getting my Masters, and he was also an up-tempo coach.

Before I present our running game and team offense, I must say that I strongly emphasize the importance of all five players on the floor. We get each player to be involved and understand his role on the break and in the offense. When everyone contributes, the result is good team spirit in addition to successful teams.

The key ingredients to a good fast break are to get all five players running and spacing the floor. One thing I was never able to do was to have a running game that designated one player to do one thing and another player to do something else in an organized fast break. It seemed like we had rules and practiced a numbered fast break but then never used it in a game.

I believe perfect practice is when you are able to do it in a game exactly as you have practiced it. So we scrapped our numbered fast break, and our fast break became "get the ball in the point guard's hands, fill the lanes, have good spacing and get everybody to the basket."

We also didn't spend time on the secondary break because, again, we didn't use it in a game. If we don't have an easy shot in transition, we just reverse the ball and get into our offense. However, we don't want to run a fast break that resembles a tennis match, back and forth ...

Our offense is based on good individual and team fundamentals like screening, cutting, movement without the ball, inside play, passing and shooting. This type of offensive structure is fun to play for every player, and the fans love it. And in this day and age with all the other things that get their adrenalin flowing in the entertainment business, our game needs to get their juices flowing too.

Occasionally (maybe three times in the roughly 63 practices we have each year), I would put an 8 to 10 minute phase in practice that I just called 'run and gun.' I'd tell them 'I want you to get the ball and go, make no more than three passes and get a good shot.' I wanted them to get tired and understand how ineffective that is over the long haul. I wanted us to run but have control. If a good shot is there, take it. If not, reverse the ball and look for a trailer. I wanted to include all five players moving down the floor and attacking the basket. I've never been a proponent of "cherry picking" or having one guy lay back because he got the rebound.

When you commit to a fast breaking style, the increased tempo requires the players to be in peak physical condition and display self-control and discipline. Possession of the ball is worth a potential four points — two that you can score and two your opponent can't score. Don't give the ball up easily — it is precious.

The building blocks of teaching an effective running game include drills where you pass well on the run, play together and get a lot of open shots.

Our drills begin with a three-man break: we rebound, outlet, get the ball to the middle and finish with a hoop. Then we go to three balls, and all three players get a shot (two players waiting with balls for the other two on the break). Next we add a defense and run our 11-man fast break drill (really continuous 3-on-2). It climaxes with team-favorite UCLA drill. The five-man running game is developed by going 5-on-0, then 5-on-2, and 5-on-3. You must emphasize that your players should ALWAYS score when numbers are in your favor.

A good 5-on-5 drill for teaching transition is to have 10 players (two groups of five) circling the free throw line. The coach throws the ball against the backboard, whichever team gets it is on offense, and the others have to get back on defense. It forces the players to change quickly from an offensive mindset, because they all want to get the ball, to defense. I believe one of the determining factors in whether you win or lose is how well your team transitions from offense to defense, especially after a turnover. You have to get back, challenge the ball, and not give up an easy lay-up.

INDIVIDUAL OFFENSE

PASSING

Passing has to be a part of every day's warm-up, and you have to make a conscious effort to compliment a good pass.

You want your players to understand and recognize, "I got the basket because of a good pass."

As legendary Princeton coach Pete Carril put it, "The quality of your passing determines the quality of your shots." Players should be able to make a chest pass, bounce pass, overhead pass and lob pass accurately. Throughout my career if there's anything that's been as important as my emphasis on defense, it's been recognizing and praising good passes and not tolerating bad passes.

There are certain times when the bounce pass is the best one to use, for example, when entering the ball to the post. On the fast break when you jump-stop at the free throw line, the bounce pass to the wing is the best.

I'm unusual in that I emphasize the two-handed overhead pass. That's the one pass I want my players to use regularly. Every day during warm-ups, we wanted them to use it on a rebound to outlet and start the fast break.

One of my favorite drills is called "star passing," which involves players following their pass. We do it with a heavy ball and then with a regular ball. The team starts by trying to go 30 seconds without a bad pass. It's never a good pass until it's completed and that takes two people. Receivers are an important part of a good pass (just like in football). Often when you are working on passing drills, players who are catching the ball can become complacent. Coaches have to emphasize and reinforce seeing the ball into their hands and catching with a jump stop so they are ready to make a move.

What I tell players about behind-the-back passes is that it's a great pass if it gets there accurately, but if it results in a turnover or it's used for showboating, they should be prepared to hear about it.

DRIBBLING

Dribbling is an overused skill in basketball. Young players often use the dribble when they aren't sure what to do with the ball.

There are two kinds of dribbles we work on: change of pace and change of direction. Each of these should be included in ball-handling practice. I de-emphasize dribbling as much as I possibly can. When all else fails, players think they can dribble, and I try to take that out of their repertoire. It's not the panacea. It becomes a BAD habit. When they don't see an open man they just put it on the floor.

Time was that moves such as going behind your back or between your legs were viewed as "hot-dogging," but today they are a recognized part of every player's dribbling repertoire. I tell my players that it's OK to use those moves if it's to gain an advantage for yourself and your team but not if you're just trying to call attention to yourself.

That's why I'm not a fan of the dribble-drive offense which is so popular now. Players in the dribble drive are taught to go and go until they're stopped, and then pass or shoot.

We would rather play three-on-three with pressure full court, then go to one dribble and then no dribbles. We play 5-man no-dribble offense at least once a week.

We think no-dribble offense helps us to move without the ball.

SHOOTING

The one individual skill most closely associated with basketball is shooting.

Youngsters pick up a ball soon after they learn how to walk and try to put the ball in the basketball hoop. As they grow up, they learn and practice a variety of shots—layups, jump shots, hook shots, free throws, driving shots and set shots. Every player, no matter how young, likes to shoot the ball.

I think good shooters are made, not born. I coached baseball a long time, and I don't think I ever made a good hitter, but I think I've made a few good shooters. I think I can make a person a good shooter—but not necessarily a great shooter—by teaching them the proper techniques and having them practice it. Because shooting techniques are hard to master, daily repetition is a must for all players.

The characteristics of a good shot are body balance and control, stance, grip, position of the elbow, position of the ball before release, sighting the basket and target area, release, follow-through, the flight arc of the ball and concentration.

There are always some players whose shots are not fundamentally sound, but they can put the ball in the basket. Craig Matthies (who is DC's all-time leading scorer), Scott Shannon, Toby Schneider and Steven Conway were all good shooters for us who didn't use classic technique.

If I work with a player in middle school, I will always try to show them the best technique. When I ran basketball camps with 4th, 5th and 6th graders I didn't spend a lot of time working on shooting because they don't have enough strength, and they were basically just throwing it up there. When they get to 7th grade you should start working on form, probably without the ball to begin with.

You owe it to every youngster to show him the correct form, but if he's a good shooter doing it his way, you just say, "Shoot it your way." Again you have to remember that the game is not about the coach, it's about the players. I can't think of anything worse than taking a player who's successful with a shot that doesn't have classic form and trying to force him to do things the "right" way. You're going to wind up with a player who still doesn't have a classic shot form but who has become a less effective shooter because of a coach's tinkering. Shooting form is one area of the game where a coach occasionally just has to stay out of his player's way.

There are many techniques for teaching shooting. Most of them break down the skill into a sequential progression that must be practiced a lot. I think it is best for players to work on their shooting by starting with short shots and progressing to longer shots. In other words, work on your form and technique close to the basket, and as you move to other shooting areas, remember to use the same techniques and shot mechanics.

There are many shooting camps around the country and each of them has a certain emphasis for shooters. I don't think teaching shooting was ever my strength, but I always had some good assistants who could do it: Andy Draayer and Ray Van Heukelem were both very good shooters and taught the fundamentals of shooting very well.

Four of the main things they emphasized which can help any shooter are:

- The release. Too many players release before they get to the top of their jump. That should be corrected.

- The follow-through. "Put it in the cookie jar" is what we say. It means to reach that shooting hand down instead of pushing it off to the side.

- The guide hand. A lot of players get it over the ball too much instead of keeping it parallel to your body at eye/ear level.

- Legs. If your shot is coming up short, bend your knees and get a little lower to keep you balanced.

One of the most effective shooting drills we used was to have the players start in one corner, move to the wing, to the top, the other wing and the other corner. They took shots inside the three-point line and had to make two in a row before they could advance to the next spot. When they made two in a row from all five spots, then could back out and shoot threes from all five spots. Making two in a row is hard for a lot of players, so it is a good drill for concentration, for shooting under pressure and for keeping a positive attitude when they miss five in a row in a game.

Another good shooting drill is shoot-and-follow with three players and two balls. You can make it competitive by using the clock.

As coaches, you can learn from their body language after they miss. Do they drop their shoulders? Do they shake their heads? Much of the time, the confidence or lack of confidence they have in their shot is at least as important as the shot mechanics. Good shooters believe every shot they take is going in.

Every player has to know his range and his area, and he has to work from there in practice. That's what we mean by shot selection. If he shoots from somewhere outside his range—and every post player thinks he is a point guard and a three-point shooter—I might let it go the first time, but if I see he's not staying with what I think is good shot selection, I'm going to tell him. You just have to demand it. After practice some players want to stay and work on their game, others just want to try to dunk. My rule was if you want to work on dunks, you have to make 10 free throws first.

I think we all resist change. I didn't like the three-point shot when it first came in, but I do now. I worked hard on the roles about who ought to be a three-pointer shooter. Now we definitely execute for a three-point shot. It's part of our offense, but it's not wise when you loft a three after the first pass. It's a great shot off the reversal but not off the first pass. If I hadn't insisted on offensive execution with my team, they would have shot more threes that twos.

SCREENING AND POSTING UP

I have always emphasized these individual offensive skills because the mastery of these fundamentals is essential to any team offense.

Screening is one of the best offensive tools in the game. Working with high school players, you don't need to make it very scientific. They should know how to pass and screen away, screen without the ball and set a stationary screen. You want to make sure everybody knows a screen is not a football block; you're just getting in the path of the defender. Players can't just run over there and stand and watch; they must get in the way.

A good part of every offense is to have a screen for the screener. Another real eye-opener is when players see how open they can be when they cut to the basket or flare to an open space after screening for a teammate.

Players must know that it's their job to use the screen—that it's not the screen that's going to get you open. Players must be taught to set up the screen with a fake and then cut off the screen as closely as they can get to the screener. If they are not doing it right, you have to stop practice and correct it because using screens effectively—both setting them and cutting off them—can be a tipping point for your offensive success.

The most important thing an inside player has to do is POST UP. I know that sounds simple but knowing how to get open in the post involves more technique than just size and strength. There are two guiding principles:

- Don't let your defender get in front of you.

- Don't move toward the wing player to get the ball. A post must stay on the block and own that spot. If he

110

moves closer to the wing, it makes it easier for the wing's defender to double team, decreases the passing angle and makes the entry pass too difficult.

Post men must work on footwork, often more than players at other positions. A lot of post men travel when they make their first move or when they pivot. I've always tried to teach every post man three really solid moves:

- Can he get it and turn around with a nice solid jump shot?

- Can he use a baby hook?

- Can he use a fake and then power up?

Feeding the post is becoming a lost art in basketball. It shouldn't be as difficult as it often seems to be. Make the first pass to the wing, take one dribble toward the baseline, and then use the bounce pass. Being able to make a lob pass is another way to get the ball inside, but teams don't work enough on that. If you don't know how to use the lob, your opponent can front the post all the time.

Throughout the years people have often talked about Denver Christian's size and how well they use the inside game. But as a coach, I have a responsibility to teach playing facing the basket to any player that I think can play at the next level. Gregg Afman, Eric Forseth, Craig Kispert, Brent Schuster and Brian Rooney all come to mind as players in the 6-4 to 6-6 range, and we needed their presence inside. We spent time with each of them on how to make a pass as well as receive one and to develop a mid-range shot. I like to have my post players able to face the basket and create for themselves.

FREE THROW SHOOTING

I regret that during my career in coaching free throw shooting has become worse while almost every other phase of the game continues to get better. That is true at every level — in the NBA, colleges and high school. It should be the easiest shot in the game—no defense, same spot on the floor in every gym in the country—but free throws can confound even the best players at times.

I wish I had a magic formula for making players better free throw shooters, but I don't. Several of our teams—including some of our champions—were only average shooters from the line.

Players are taught the proper fundamentals and get plenty of repetitions. Yet the downhill trend continues. A lot of it is mental, and that's hard to teach—it has to do with pressure and presence. A coach must teach them to focus and always shoot the ball the same way. It's a good idea to vary the situations when you have your players shoot them. For example, it's important to have them shoot with tired legs to get used to shooting late in the game. You also need to make it a competition, e.g., a sprint for every miss, one player shoots and the entire team has to run if he misses.

You can change their feet, their shoulders and their elbow position, but I never let them shoot differently because they missed. In a perfect world you would like to have them come out of the summer with their free throw technique in place, but kids will fiddle with their mechanics, imitate somebody they've seen on television or just change because of frustration.

If someone is really struggling, you should just try to reinforce the basics: bend your knees and hold your follow-through.

Nothing you can say is going to matter. So much of it is mental. Some kids believe every shot is going to go in. With others you can see they're struggling every time they go to the line. I never wanted to say "Make this one" or "We need this." When a shooter has to go to the line after a timeout, you should never say a thing to him during the timeout. Sometimes you don't even want to look at him. Don't dwell on it.I do think it's a good idea to step off the line after a miss just to reset their mechanics.

How important are free throws? When you're fouled shooting, and you miss both free throws, that's a turnover. It's one of the little things that can make the difference between a champion and a challenger.

TEAM OFFENSE

Great offense is characterized by the proper execution of fundamentals and being willing to sacrifice. A team player's total contribution is best measured by making the offense move (passing), refusing to dominate play (excessive dribbling) and by the quality shots you attempted from natural movement (shot selection).

There will always be flavors-of-the-month offenses, but it is important to find a system that is flexible enough to fit the changes in personnel a coach is going to have over the years. Don't ever use an offense this year because it worked last year. Be flexible and adjust the system to fit your team's strengths. Your offense is also something that you have to believe in and, most importantly, that you can teach and "sell" to your players.

When I came to Denver Christian, we had a very good team with two solid inside players. We always wanted to get the ball inside or run with the ball. But about the second or third year, Air Academy High School was on our schedule.

Bob Spear was the coach at the Air Force Academy, and his son played there. They ran a continuity offense, known as the Air Force Shuffle. I thought we were a good defensive team, but we couldn't stop it. I decided to implement the continuity into our offensive structure—at least our players would learn how to play against it in practice.

The goal was to come up with an offense that had structure but incorporated the principles of motion. Rightly or wrongly I wanted to know where the players were expected to be on each possession. If there aren't any definite assignments on offense, players seem to do their own thing. That's the motion offense that is still very popular today. But under pressure players tend to lose consistency of movement and become confused. Instead of grabbing things from here and there, we needed something that incorporated our philosophy and style.

We went to something we call Alabama (see chapter 11), which can be run from a 1-2-2 set or a 1-4 set. This offense has become the Denver Christian trademark offensively—everyone (players, opponents and probably some of our fans) knows what we are going to do when we say "BAMA." We have used it (with several variations) for the past 20-plus years.

The offense begins with an entry pass (or dribble) to the wing, a post-up low ball-side, and a screen away following the pass. There is good spacing, and when the ball is reversed, continuity results. When we had a strong inside player who could post-up, we would enter to him and let him go "one on one" inside because all the other action was away from the ball.

If we are patient and reverse the ball, we don't need to have a separate offense for the last two minutes—we simply reverse the ball and limit our shot selection to layups. Early in the season we probably run "BAMA" 70 percent of the time on offense. Our players believe in it because they have been running it since they entered the program. In crucial situations they will say "Lets run BAMA" as Riley Herren did in the last two and a half minutes of the state championship game against Limon in 2012.

In the early 2000s we added a set, which we call "Duke," (see chapter 12). The Matthies twins, Tristan and Cameron, were excellent three-point shooters on teams that won back-to-back titles for us. Their father, Craig, was on our first undefeated team.

I had seen Duke University run something for J.J. Redick involving the pick-and-roll and a 3-point shot, and we adapted their play to use one twin to come off the pick and the other twin to drain a three.

The wing has the ball; the post man sets a screen for him and rolls to the basket. As the wing came off the screen, help defense was needed and that freed up the other wing.

Every team should have a simple pass and cut offense, which spreads the floor against a team that is trying to pressure the ball and trap but probably doesn't know how to defend against good screens and cuts. We have an offense called WHEEL that can be used against this.

We also drill weekly for when a team gets in your face offensively. We teach players to make long pivots away from the defender and to "sweep with the ball." We practice this in a 15-foot square area and go 3-on-3. We work very hard on those long pivots, sweeping the ball and how to defend a player who does them. It's not easy to teach, so you have to be patient. We would have five veteran players demonstrate it, and let them teach it to the younger players. It is good reinforcement for the idea that your older players have to be teachers and models for the ones coming up behind them.

Our zone offense is run with the same floor alignment as our man-to-man offense. We set up with a one guard (1-2-2, 1-3-1, or 1-4) if the opposition is playing a two-guard front zone, and in a two-guard front (2-1-2 or 2-3) against a zone with one guard at the top.

The most basic zone offense we run is called KANSAS (see Kansas diagrams in chapter 13), which has wings cutting through and post men high and low. Most people think the only way to beat a zone is with outside shooting, but it's possible to get good inside shots with reversals and ball movement with this offense.

Ideally, before you play your first game you would like to have two man-to-man offenses and two zone offenses that your players believe in and can execute well. In addition, each player should have the flexibility to play at least two positions on each offense.

Every team I've coached has also known how to run the flex offense, because I want our players to be able to defend it. The truth is I'd be surprised if we ran it 10 times a year, but it's a nice set to have available to change things up, e.g., running it for one possession coming out of a timeout to see if you can catch the defense off guard and get a quick basket.

POINT GUARDS

A good point guard is the position a team must have in order to perform well — the good teams have good point guards. I've often said, "Point guards are made in heaven." By that I mean I don't know that I have ever taken a guard and coached him into a great point guard—one who is able to make good choices, doesn't force it and is in control of the game.

Guy Gibbs, a good friend who had an outstanding record at Regis Jesuit High School, used to say, "I want my point guard to get the ball across half court, get us into our offense and not care if he ever gets the ball back."

Riley Herren, the point guard on my last team, only averaged two shots a game, but we wanted the ball in his hands.If a player got open Riley would reward him—he was exactly what you would want in a point guard. It is a bonus if a point guard can shoot, but I think he should shoot only after he gives it up and gets it back. The most important thing your point guard should do is to maximize the performance of the other players around him. He is the leader whose job it is to know everyone else's roles and get them involved.

Throughout the years our good teams invariably featured good point guards. Jim De Groot, who was the best player I ever coached, was able to play any position on the floor, but when he played point guard he made everyone better. He went on to play at Phillips University in Enid, OK and then to Hawaii-Hilo in the 80's.

Bobby Tamminga from the 1990-92 teams is another point guard who led Denver Christian to the state finals. He then played at Northwest Nazarene University in Nampa, ID. The Vriesman brothers, Josh and Jacob, were both outstanding point guards and leaders for Denver Christian. Both of them played basketball and baseball at Calvin College, my alma mater.

END OF GAME STRATEGY

If we are ahead in a close game and the game is winding down, the team must be coached on what to do. My end of game philosophy for the last two minutes is to shoot only lay-ups and free throws and take care of the ball.

Many times my team didn't do that very well, probably because we were an up-tempo team and I was coaching them to slow down. I think I would alter my view on that if I were starting over, and just continue to play "our game."

I don't think we presently need a shot clock in high school basketball because very few teams try to hold the ball. I think the shot clock will come to high school basketball in the future (there are some states that have already enacted it), and its emergence would definitely impact the strategy at the end of the game.

It is crucial at all times, and especially in the final minutes of a close game, to keep your players focused during long possessions. Many good things happen if they are patient and don't force things. The upside is that the defending team will get anxious and take chances. The downside is that the offense is more likely to take a bad shot or make a turnover. You prepare your team for that in practice by insisting they make seven passes before they take a shot. They must know that if they are disciplined and patient, the defense will get lazy and your team can take advantage of that.

BREAK A PRESS

When your team has to break a press, the most important player is the one who inbounds the ball. Choose this player carefully. He should be one who sees the court well, doesn't panic, makes good choices on reversal passes and long passes down court and has some size.

His teammates must know how to get open by using good screens and sharp cuts. We use our big man to set a screen for the point guard, then he moves down court to become a deep outlet target.

It is best if the players 1 and 2 (your guards) receive the ball, reverse through the in-bounder, and slash to the middle and down court. Of course, if the player at half-court is open, it's a no-brainer to hit him and attack the basket. This is a five-person attack unless it's just man-for-man pressure. Against that kind of press we just get the ball in the hands of the point guard and get out of his way.

117

Chapter 11: Alabama

Alabama has become our offensive trademark. We can run it either from a 1-2-2 set or a 1-4.

The offense begins with an entry pass (or dribble) to the wing, a post-up low ball-side, and a screen away following the pass. There is good spacing, and when the ball is reversed, continuity results. When we had a strong inside player who could post-up, we would enter to him and let him go "one on one" inside because all the other action was away from the ball.

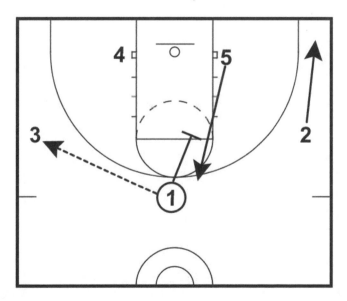

Figure A: 1 passes to 3, then moves to screen for 5 just below the free throw line. 5 moves up the lane to the top of the key—this is close to a moving screen but the point must make sure he does not contact 5's defender while he (1) is moving. It doesn't have to be a full screen, just enough to free 5 to get to the top of the key. 2 moves toward the baseline and the post on ball side posts up hard.

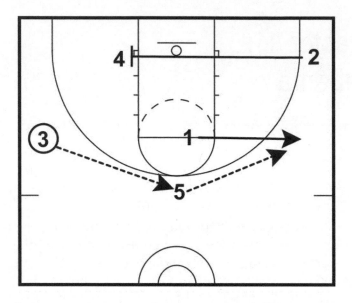

Figure B: 1 reverse pivots out to the wing as 5 comes off his screen. 3 passes to 5, who immediately reverses to 1. 2 screens opposite low post on the air time of the pass from 3 to 5.

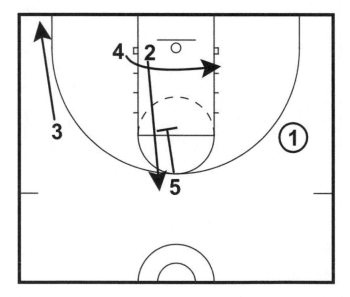

Figure C: On the pass to 1, low post 4 cuts either above or below 2's screen; this is the first option. 5 moves to screen just below the free throw line for 2 who cuts off the screen to the point; this is the second option. 3 moves to the baseline and 5 reverse pivots to the wing to take the reversal pass. Play is now continuous until it produces and open shot.

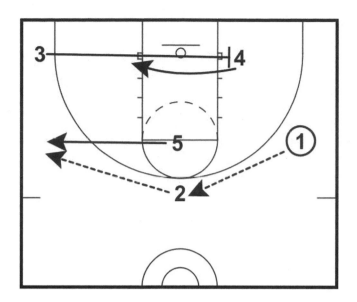

Figure D: The reset: 2 is now the point and receives the pass from 1. The ball is immediately reversed to 5 who has reverse-pivoted to the wing. 3 screens across on the airtime of the pass from 1 to 2 and the play is continuous.

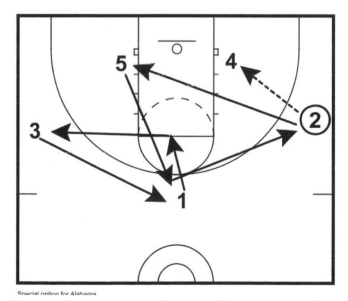

Special option for Alabama

Special option for Alabama — Post entry from wing
On any pass from wing to a low post, the wing must cut immediately to the opposite block. The other players rotate as shown. 5 flashes to the top of the key, then replaces 3 on the wing. 3 comes up to replace 5 at the top as 1 makes an "L" cut to replace 3 on the wing.

Chapter 12:
Duke

I had seen Duke University run something for J.J. Redick involving the pick-and-roll and a 3-point shot. I thought the Matthies twins could fit those roles perfectly — Cameron coming off the pick and Tristan the three-point shooter. We have used Duke as part of our offensive arsenal ever since.

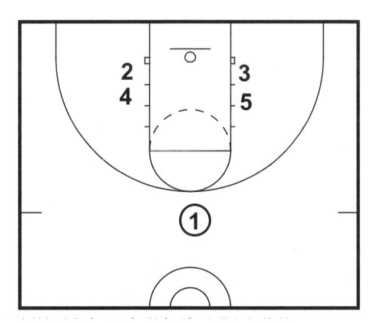

Figure A: 1 brings the ball to the frontcourt, 2 and 4 are stacked on one low block, 3 and 5 are stacked on the other.

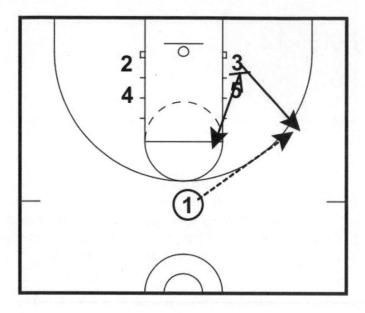

Figure B: 3 gets a screen from 5 and pops to the wing to receive a pass from 1. After screening, 5 reverse pivots to the high post.

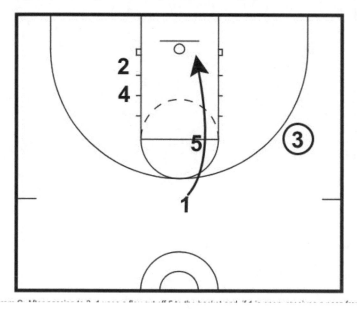

Figure C: After passing to 3, 1 uses a flex cut off 5 to the basket and if 1 is open, receives a pass from 3 for a layup. If 1 doesn't receive the pass, he fills to the opposite corner.

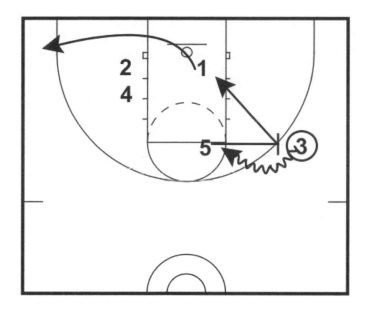

Figure D: 5 and 3 run a traditional pick and roll. 3 drives as far as he can go. Often, he is stopped by help from 2's defender. 5 rolls to the basket.

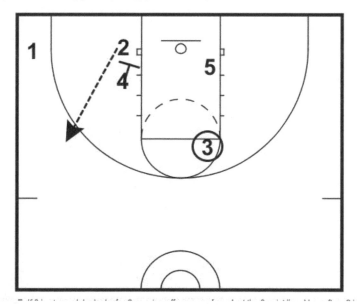

Figure E: If 3 is stopped, he looks for 2 coming off a screen from 4 at the 3-point line. Very often, 2 is wide open for a three-point shot.

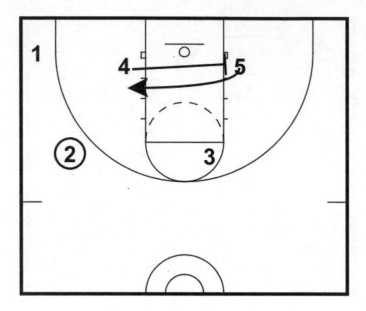

Figure F: After screening for 2, 4 continues across the lane to set a screen for 5, who cuts across the lane. Following these options, if nothing has created an open shot, we are set up to run our motion offense.

Chapter 13:
Kansas

The most basic zone offense we run is called Kansas, which has wings cutting through and post men high and low. Many people think the only way to beat a zone is with outside shooting but it's possible to get good inside shots with reversals and ball movement with this offense.

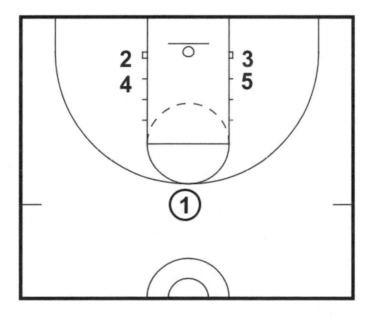

Figure A: 1 brings the ball to the top of the zone. Ideally, the point guard stays in the middle of the floor. 2 and 4 are stacked on one block, 3 and 5 on the other.

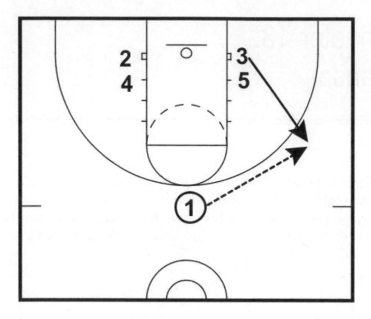

Figure B: 3 flashes to the wing to receive a pass from 1.

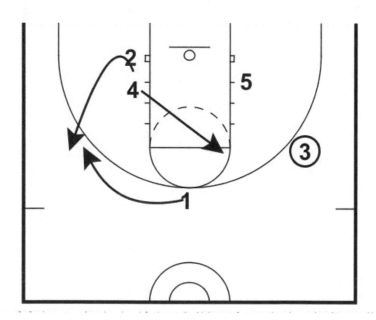

Figure C: On the pass to 3 on the wing, 4 flashes to the high post, 2 cuts to the wing and exchanges with 1.

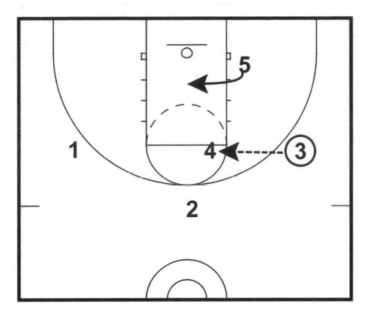

Figure D: 3 looks for 4 at the high post (not an option that is often open). If the pass is made, 5 ducks in to look for a pass from 4.

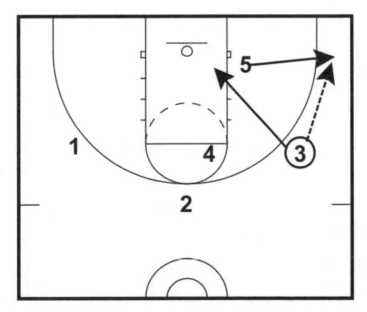

Figure E: 5 cuts to the corner (not the short corner) to receive a pass from 3, who replaces 5 on the low post.

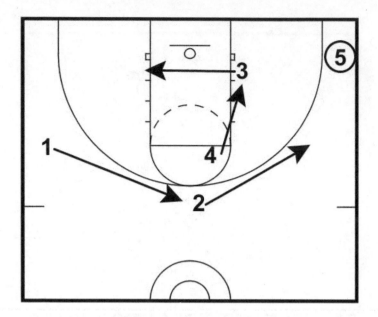

Figure F: 2 moves to the wing and is replaced at the top by 1. 3 moves to the opposite block and is replaced on the low block by 4. 5 can pass to 4 on the block or reverse the ball to 2.

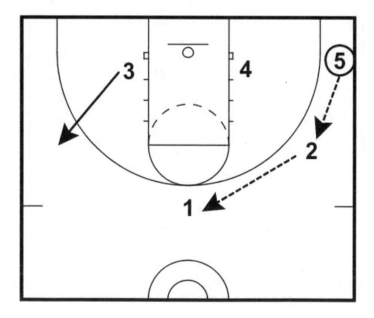

Figure G: 5 reverses the ball to 2. On the reversal, 4 traces every pass looking for an opening in the lane, ideally finishing on the opposite block. If 2 cannot pass inside, he reverses the ball to 1. As 1 receives the ball, 3 pops to the three-point line. 5 replaces 4 on the low block.

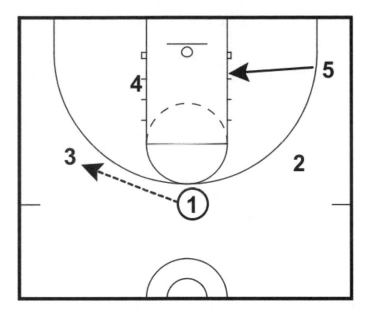

Figure H: If no one is open, we have had a complete reversal and the ball can be entered by 1 to start the action. Reversals are key to attacking a zone and this encourages continuous ball reversal.

Chapter 14: Practice— Where Good Technique is Taught and Bad Habits are Broken

Practice is where the seeds of fundamentals, teamwork and discipline are sown. These are enriched with competitiveness, repetition and sportsmanship to produce young people who will be successful basketball players — and have fun doing it.

Since every coach is a teacher, he must realize and use the many teachable moments that occur during practice and games. In the excitement and intensity of competition, coaches must work to be even-tempered and rational. They are in an arena where emotions get out of hand many times. The coach must not get caught up in this.

A coach earns respect and accolades from well-coached games, but he earns his credibility in well-coached practices. Any coach who does not love to go to practice probably doesn't belong in coaching and will not have long-term success. The word "love" is used intentionally because practice is where your work is done. It is where you have to prepare your hardest, give your best effort and impose the structure that makes teams successful. When players catch that "fever" from the coach, the results are a positive experience for all.

During my 48 years as head coach at Denver Christian, I coached 1109 varsity basketball games. However, I have conducted roughly 3500 practices.

Victories are gained and state championships are won on Saturdays in large arenas, but they are earned on weekday afternoons in empty gyms.

Every season is different because every team is different. At the beginning of each season a coach needs to make a plan of all the things he wants the team to be able to accomplish. Dream a little, but temper the dream with reality. Never use the plans from last year for this year's team. God never intended us to live today in the same way we did yesterday. The long-range plans will need some adjusting but they serve as a reference so that nothing will be overlooked as the season progresses.

I can't imagine any coach going into a practice without a very specific plan. That is, knowing exactly what he or she needs to accomplish and how they are going to accomplish it.

Formal practice plans take many forms. Some coaches use computer printouts based on a template that allows you to input the times and activities, others use index cards or small notebooks. What is important is that you use a method that is familiar and comfortable for you. One thing I would caution about using a computer template is that while it is easy, it becomes tempting to use the same timeframe today as you did yesterday and this year can become the same as last year.

I almost always used a hand-written schedule on a single piece of 8½ by 11-inch paper. I've found that I think more clearly when I am physically devising a plan by writing down every word and number by hand. This is probably due to my math background. Also, there were no personal computers when I started coaching and teaching.

I still have paper copies of virtually every practice schedule from the last 39 years. If the team is having the same trouble with an aspect of the game that a team from five years ago had, it can be helpful to go back and see how I dealt with it then.

Reviewing my practice plan from the beginning of the season also points out what facets of the game I may be over-emphasizing or under-emphasizing. Going back a few years may help you remember the drills used to develop skills and/or situations that you have neglected for awhile.

Rarely do I post the practice schedule on the wall or even let my players see it. I don't want players anticipating what is next, rather than focusing on the task before them—like trying to get through the defensive drills so we can play "cutthroat." The assistants received their copies before practice.

Assistant coaches always have input on my practice schedule, and players occasionally did. I like to ask, "What else do you think we need more of?" so my assistants and players can feel part of the plans. It also helps build a sense of trust and importance. If one of the captains makes a good suggestion I will likely mention during practice that "We are doing this today because 'A' thought we needed to work on it."

Reproduced on the following page is the schedule for the 19th practice of the 2011-12 season, during which the team went undefeated and won the state championship.

We have begun practice with the DC Warmup for at least the last 10 years. I believe you should have a name for your warmup and drills so you can call it out and your players can jump to position.

Your warmup should include what is vital to your program and prepare your players for practice.

In our DC Warmup we have two lines 15 feet apart and the players make chest passes to their partner all the way down the floor. At the end of the floor the players flow to the sideline and come back down the floor throwing 40-foot overhead passes. What you wind up with is almost a tunnel: One set of players is making 15-foot chest passes underneath the overhead passes thrown by the players on the outside.

I am one of a few coaches who believe very strongly in the overhead pass. Along with the lob, it is one of the least-practiced passes but I believe they are vital. We want to use an overhead pass off every rebound and when we are being pressed. You can snap it and throw it further with accuracy than any other pass.

After the passing segment we move into a variety of full-court drills that emphasize passing, dribbling and shooting. I always wanted to vary the exact nature of the drills a little so your players are learning the same skills but not performing them in exactly the same way every day. It keeps them from getting stale and from starting to cut corners because they are so familiar with the drill.

Most days we did a two-man outlet/rebound/layup drill that reinforces the most important skills in our transition offense.

One player tosses the ball off the backboard then rebounds it, pivots and makes an overhead pass to the wing near the sideline at the free throw line extended. The wing dribbles to the middle of the floor and continues to the free throw line where he jump stops and makes a bounce pass—and the bounce pass is cru-

2011 - 2012

PRACTICE # 19
Wed, Dec. 7
2:50 - 4:40
With Intensity
Build momentum

DENVER
CHRISTIAN
CRUSADER BASKETBALL

2:50 - 3:05	Warmup
	DC +
3:05 - 3:12	30 sec. drills
3:12 - 3:21	3's
3:21 - 3:25	3 on 3 rush pressure
	(so its 3on2 ⟹ 3on3) defender of one who
	gets ball - touch
3:25 - 3:40	Zone Rehearsal - Run
	23 ⟹ Kansas + Jayhawks
	13 ⟹ Ram + Wyoming
	14 ⟹ Carolina or box
3:40 - 3:45	Pressing - 12 /slash
	tempo - no layups
3:45 - 4:00	M 4 M — change ends
	Carolina - Bama - Duke - wheel (7 passes)
	no shot unless post touches
4:00 - 4:10	FT - 2's - never
4:10 - 4:20	Big - Little
	power lays 22 - 1on1 - 1on2 - runnin
	re couns - 3 optin + handles
4:20 - 4:32	Offense for 14
	Zone OB
4:32 - 4:40	Shooting
	2 in row 4 min
	10 spots
	Run —

Tomorrow - South
Eligibility

Begin prep - sleep
ATTITUDE!

Christmas - scrimmage
— Party

136

The object of this drill is for Chris Pranger (coming around a chair with assistant coach Andy Draayer seated in it) to catch up to dribbler Rafael Luna before he gets a layup. Photographer Craig Vanden Heuvel shoots the action for Root Sports and assistant coach Steve Herrerma is in the background.

cial—to the rebounder who has sprinted hard to fill the lane. While one set of players is running the two-man break on the right side of the floor, another is running it on the left side.

We are very demanding of the way they execute this drill, from the pivot to the overhead pass to the jump stop and pass. Over the years I've become convinced that the emphasis we put on this drill is a among the main reasons why we have had so many point guards who would make the jump stop and look for a finisher.

Next we would run a continuous three-man weave with several variations. Sometimes they run the traditional weave, sometimes they stay in lanes, and sometimes we make it a five-man weave.

Most teams run the "3-on-2 down, 2-on-1 back" drill because you can tell a lot about your players by the way they respond in these situations. Will they sprint as hard back on defense as they did on offense? Can they stop penetration without fouling or giving up an easy pass? The two things we emphasize are no turnovers and how to defend when you are outnumbered. Players need to understand that two can defend three if they *anticipate* and make the ball be passed more than twice.

We teach the first player to stop the ball at the top of the key and the second player to play the first pass. Then the first player drops to pick up the second pass. The point of emphasis is "NO LAYUPS."

When they come back 2-on-1 we want the defensive player to be able to sprint to half-court in two or three big steps, then pivot and find the ball. I'm not adamant about whether the defensive player backpedals or runs forward as he gets back to his basket as long as he doesn't lose sight of the ball.

We can run numerous varieties of this drill as well: make it a five-man-weave down and 3-on-2 back, or a three-man-weave down, then 2 on 1 back. Shaking things up is one of the reasons my teams didn't get stale in February or March.

We are a small school and all of our players—from freshmen to seniors—participated in DC Warmup together. Some of our young players are going to get lost during the warmup drills early in the season but that gives our older players a chance to teach and lead by example.

After the warmup we move into our 30-second drills on alternate days. On this day we did two of them: the Mikan drill and timed shooting. We use a number of variations on the timed shooting: elbow-to-elbow jump shots, layups from the elbow and two-ball power layups in which we put a ball on each block and the player must pick it up, pivot and score. We establish a standard for each of those and it increases as the season progresses.

The "3's" drill is something we often do. I've always said that if I were going to reinvent the game of basketball I would make it 3-on-3. If they can play well 3-on-3, then 5-on-5 is easy. Everyone is involved in 3-on-3, there aren't players away from the ball. It incorporates screening, cutting, help, recovery and every concept of the game.

Two days before a game for the last 30 or 35 years we've played 3-on-2 to seven possessions. We pick two guys to play defense and see how many stops they can get. We frown on turnovers when you have an advantage. The offensive players have to see the open man and hustle. It emphasizes passing and timing and rebounding.

On this day we used another 3-on-3 drill called "Rush." A coach passes the ball to an offensive player and his defender must go and touch the baseline before he can defend.

Every drill has to be based on the fundamentals of the game. I'm a sequential guy so I like to go from 3-on-3 to 4-on-4 and then to the competitive situations of 5-on-5.

With this sample schedule, we were three weeks into the season so we spent 15 minutes on our basic offenses and defenses, then five minutes working on our press.

This point in practice is when we often shot free throws. They've been working hard, their legs are a little tired just as they would be in a game. It's repetition surrounded by running. I don't think you ever want them to stand there and shoot more than two in a row. I've ended many practices where I got to pick a player and the team got to pick a player and one player would volunteer. They had to make both ends of a one-and-one or the whole team ran. Sometimes I went through the whole roster on a Monday or Tuesday to get some conditioning. They know I'm going to pick a poor free throw shooter and they're going to pick a good one.

"Big-Little" is something we do a couple of times a week. We divide up to work on skills specific to position and size: posting up, the baby hook, the turnaround jump shot for the big players; dribbling, shooting and ball handling for the guards.

The "12" designates our 1-2-2 press. "Slash" is what we run against it; we reverse the ball and slash down the middle.

"M4M" means man for man. Monday is when we worked on defense. Tuesday was our offensive day.

The shooting drill we used on this day is making two in a row from 10 different spots.

I tried to end each practice with something competitive and fun. Sometimes we would choose three guys to shoot free throws. If we make them, we smile. If we don't, we run. I try to send them home feeling pretty good about themselves.

Some coaches view their practice plans as a sketch/outline and improvise as necessary when their team needs more or less work on some specific aspect of the game. Over the years I've been an advocate of sticking to my original plan and trying not to deviate more than five minutes from that original schedule.

The time frames for each segment of my practice schedule are neither arbitrary nor capricious. For example, over the years I've determined that seven minutes—not six or eight—is the correct duration for one specific drill. I'm not sure I can explain exactly why, but if you coach long enough you develop an instinct for these things.

I also came to believe in what I might call, "Quitting while you're behind." By that I mean that if your players just aren't getting something, it can become counter-productive to keep going over and over it. Call it off and come back to it the next day. It took me about 15 years to learn to use a different approach when something was going badly. I think this is a hard concept for a lot of coaches to grasp, but it is very important for a young coach to learn—don't wait 15 years to learn it. I will put it away, save it for another day and consider that maybe the way I'm teaching it is part of the problem. If I'm going to second-guess my players for not learning, I shouldn't be afraid to second-guess the way I'm teaching it. The advantage to this is that it takes away the mental attitude that says, "We can't do this anyhow" so I can come back and say, "I want you to learn this, but let's try it this way."

I use a whistle during practice. I know some coaches don't use them, but I've found it valuable if used discretely. I also believe players must get used to responding to the sound of my voice. I try to use my voice mostly for teaching and encouraging and for criticism only if constructive. Players must realize that when I say "Freeze" or use my whistle that means, "Stop right where you are" but both the whistle and the voice can be misused in practice. One thing I was a stickler about is I never let players sit down in practice, for the simple reason that it takes you longer to get up and get into a drill instead of just jumping in from the sideline.

I believe teams need to work every day on *special situations* they may encounter in a game. These situations include out-of-bounds plays, time and score scenarios and how to play from behind or ahead. I feel I have failed my team as a coach if they encountered something in a game I had not prepared them for in practice.

We work on our baseline out of bounds against a man and a zone and how to defend them regularly. Many times I can use these on the sideline against pressure. Many situations become special when you use the clock and the score.

We regularly practiced what we called "Time and Score." For us that meant less than 30 seconds in the quarter, we had the ball and wanted to score without giving our opponent an opportunity to score. The ideal situation was for us to run some clock, start a play at :08 and get a shot at :03. The best-case scenario is we make a three-point basket and time runs out. If we miss, nothing is lost because the buzzer sounds on the rebound.

The worst case is to "lose points" in time and score. That could happen if we shot the ball too early and the opponent had a chance to score, or if we committed a turnover when we were using the clock.

Some of the other examples of "Time and Score" we practiced for include:

- Up 3 with 2 minutes left in the half;
- Down 2 with 1 minute left in the game (when and who to foul).
- Up or down 5 points with 3 minutes left in the game.
- Our ball, 10 seconds left in the period.
- Our ball, 5 seconds left in the period.

Although it is rare to change your starters from game to game, it is important that each player believes he has a fair chance. You should vary the combinations of players competing together throughout practice. You don't want an 'us-vs. them" team. Every player should be included in rotations and every player must understand his role. This can only happen with proper planning and teaching during practice. Every player must be hungry and know that he will get his chance in every practice and every game.

As the season goes on, my starters play together more as the players start to separate. Even then, every player must know his role.

The coach's position on the court during practice is important. I want to greet the players when they arrive and move around so I can get to all players and all places on the court. I know I see different things from every position so I constantly move around. When on the baseline I get a good look at inside play and how players react after a pass. At half court, the play on the perimeter is right in front of me and the spacing and footwork are readily visible.

I wrote daily affirmations on each day's schedule to remind both the team and myself of the overall emphases that were within our grasp and what it would take to achieve them..

Things like:

"Forever Moments."

"Seize the opportunity."

"Savor the moment."

"Our last week together."

"Focus. Prepare. Enjoy."

"Yesterday's Scrimmage."

"Use it for Momentum."

"We move forward! And Stay Humble."

"Time to Step Up" "Want It."

"Hungry. No egos."

"Poised. Disciplined. Positive."

"No more easy ones. Step it up."

"Attitude/Commitment/Believe/Trust."

"Last week of league. Seniors, step up!"

"Let's Add a Couple of Things."

"Work Hard. We Must Make Each Other Better."

"No Shortcuts."

"Become Better Shooters."

"Trust."

Coaches have to be very attentive to the rhythm of their practice. Just like good music, a good practice has a very specific ebb and flow with periods of intensity followed by calmer segments. Not only do the players need time to recover physically, but if you keep raising the intensity level, either through more physical drills or the way you are interacting with them, you will find your team getting too caught up in the emotion and losing focus on

This is the schedule for our 45th practice of the season. Some things are always there, others have gained more sophistication as the season goes on.

2011 – 2012

DENVER CHRISTIAN

CRUSADER BASKETBALL

PRACTICE # 45
THURS, FEB. 9
2:50 — 4:30
TURN it up a NOT
"Mr. Crusader" in Spot!

2:55 — 3:12	WARM UP 2 lines — 3 ball - DC / 3's
3:12 — 3:15	SHOOTING shot fake
3:15 — 3:25	3 man stuff – entries – post exchange – perimeter – zone (inside 3 pt)
3:25 — 3:40	ZONE DEFENSE 2 3 / ∆ + 2 (what offense)
3:40 - 3:48	FREE Throws (2)
3:48 - 3:50	PRESSURE MyM — 10 – gotten a little soft
3:50 — 4:00	5 on 5 (6's) Carolina / Florida
4:00 - 4:05	ADVANTAGE
4:05 - 4:15	NEW — UTah
4:15 - 4:23	more shooting
4:23 - 4:30	3 man games —

Tomorrow — with girls / Mr. Crusader / Hoe-down
" you haven't won anything yet" ! (month
Saturday — 11 / 12:30 / 2 — white again

143

the details. Intersperse the most physical drills with a few minutes of skill drills or just give them a water break.

My critics might say that because of what I demanded in the individual drills and the early part of practice, the last 30 minutes wasn't as intense as the first part.

That's probably right but I always felt it was important to teach the fundamentals in the beginning when the players are fresh and ready to learn. My drills were always sequential with one thing leading to something more demanding: three-on-three, four-on-four, and cutthroat. We had breakdown drills for each offense — they were the parts that formed the whole.

I believe you should introduce new things — a fresh wrinkle on offense, a new out-of-bounds play or a tweak to your defense — when you transition from individual drills to 5-on-5 work. You should then reinforce them before the end of practice so you have a better chance of them carrying over to the next day.

I had a reputation as a disciplinarian, especially early in my career, but it was more that I wanted to instill a sense of discipline in my practices. Things can go downhill very quickly when teenage boys get the idea that they can cut corners. No Shortcuts! That said, it is counterproductive to be so rigid and autocratic that you take the fun out of the game.

Don't overload players with rules. I did have a couple of things I insisted upon during practice: Never sit down and always have proper practice equipment. I don't want them coming to practice without a reversible and proper gear. Don't talk when I'm talking. Stop on the whistle. Always be on time!

Many coaches, perhaps even most coaches, don't allow parents to attend their practice. I do.

In order to create a sense of community, I didn't feel right banning them, especially if they were there to pick up their youngsters.

When we started our program we relied on the parents to do a lot of things and they were very supportive. I let them sit in practice but they can't talk to their son and there were only certain times (never during practice, sometimes after practice) when they could talk to me. I never reached the point where I thought they shouldn't be there. Besides, some of those dads played for me.

No matter how organized and efficient I became at devising optimum practice schedules, my team still is going to have bad practices. Good teams will have fewer bad practices than mediocre teams but even our championship teams have had at least one or two days when my assistants and I have looked at each other and shook our heads. There were a few times when we just ended practice and told them to regroup tomorrow.

The reasons for a bad practice are many: I may have prepared a practice schedule that kept my team from establishing a rhythm. I am as self-critical as most coaches, but most of the time that doesn't happen.

I think it is more the nature of the environment. You are dealing with high school students. They may not be feeling well. Aside from hospitals, high schools may be the most germ-friendly environment on earth. Kids are often sniffling, coughing, sneezing or afflicted with some other malady. The most disease-prone times of the year tend to be in mid-December when you are near the holidays and at the end of the semester when stress is high; and late January when your players may be starting to get worn down physically by the grind of the season. If players aren't healthy, no amount of will or encouragement can get them to perform at a high level.

They may also be suffering from a variety of outside influences: girlfriend trouble; assignments hanging over their heads; issues at home. It only takes a couple of your better players performing listlessly in practice for the entire team to be infected.

Some coaches let their players come in for gym time on their own, but unless there is a coach present it is usually wasted time. Players can learn bad habits without coaching instead of working on their skills. That's the great thing about basketball. You don't need anyone to catch your throws, pitch to you or kick the ball to you. If you have a ball, a hoop and the will, you can make yourself a better player.

The same thing applies when players go to rec centers or gyms. Few of them can resist the temptation to play pick-up games in favor of going off by themselves to work on their skills.

Film and video review can be valuable but it can also be overused. Early in the season I almost always show the film from the game before. If we play on Friday we come in Saturday or Monday and look at film. I learned that after the fifth or sixth game, they're looking at the wrong things: making fun of somebody or just not paying attention.

At that point it becomes something we do for the really important games and when we get into the playoffs and are playing a team we haven't seen. One of your players might ask to take a game film home to review it, and I always let them, but it's hard to know if they've gotten anything out of it.

I live near a college and have profited by attending their practices and games. If there is a person you admire, ask to attend a couple of his practices or games. I don't know of any college coach who won't open the doors for a high school coach. I'm really not trying so much to absorb what the coach teaches (although I almost always come away with a drill or a play that fits my team), I'm just trying to absorb HOW he teaches it. If possible, attend more than one practice and spend at least one of them NOT scribbling notes but rather watching and listening to absorb the ambience and atmosphere a successful coach establishes to maximize the learning environment.

I have touched on some of these issues elsewhere in this book but I felt it was important to bring them all together in one chapter because I believe nothing is more important, especially for a young coach, than learning how to plan, structure and execute a successful practice.

The basic components of every practice should be proper warmup, drills for fundamentals, repetition of skills, shooting, breakdown drills, offensive team play, defensive team play and special situations.

I would encourage any coach who doesn't look forward to going to practice to do some self-analysis, ask himself/herself why he or she is in the game. It's a teacher/coach's delight to have two hours daily of a young person's life to teach, correct, establish relationships and develop character. It is the ultimate educational opportunity, and you don't want to waste it.

Chapter 15:
Press Break

Our press break against a zone press is called Slash. It requires movement and a precise series of cuts (slashes) to open areas.

As I progressed through my coaching years, I felt my teams were difficult to press because we had practiced how to attack a press regularly and believed we would get the ball upcourt and get a good shot from our attack. It must be realized that if the press is man-for-man, we like the ball in the hands of our best ball-handler — if it is a zone press we ran SLASH. Again we like the ball to be thrown in by player 4 (3), and every pass is followed by a "slash to the basket." Player 4 inbounds the ball and is the reversal man in the attack. The reversal from side to side continues until we obtain an advantage – like 3 on 1, or 4 on 2.

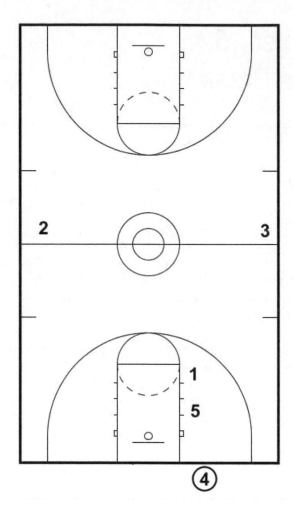

Figure A: Ideally, the 4 man inbounds the ball, making sure not to be directly below the basket. 1 and 5 are a step apart, either on the lane or at the free throw line.

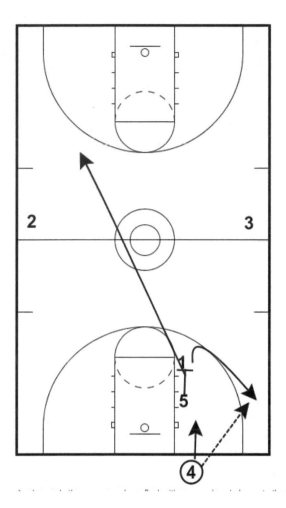

Figure B: 5 screens 1, who reads the screen and can flash either way, almost always to the ball side and being mindful not to go too deep into the corner. As 1 receives the ball, 4 steps inbounds and 5 goes up the floor in a "basketball gait," running under control and always able to receive a pass.

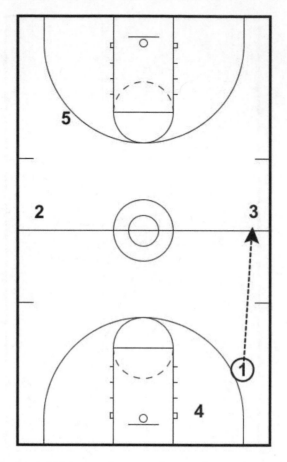

Figure C: Option 1: If 3 is open for a pass from 1, the press is broken and 3 attacks the basket in a three-man fast break. Usually, this pass is not available but it is important that 1 uses a ball-fake towards 3 to make the defense honor the threat.

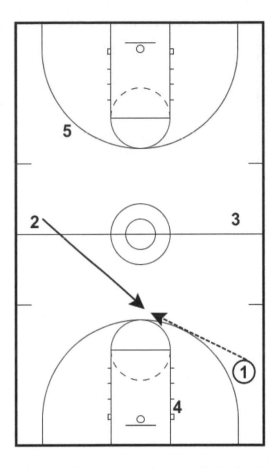

Figure D: Second option: If the pass to 3 is not available, 2 makes a diagonal cut to the top of the key to receive a pass from 1 and turns to attack the basket with 5 and 3.

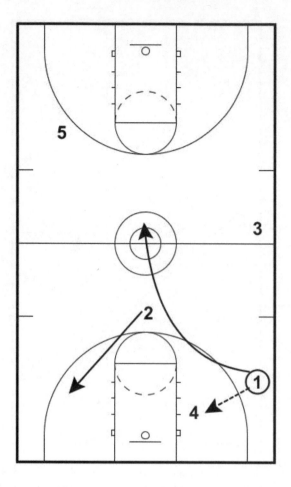

Figure E: Option 3: If 2 does not receive the ball, 2 vacates to the opposite side. 1 passes to 4 and slashes across half court.

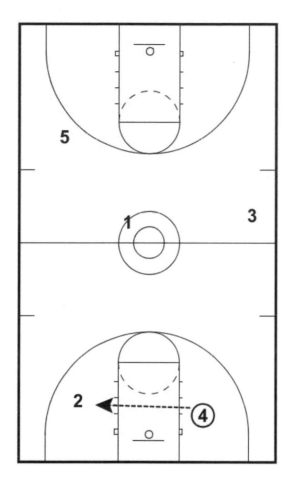

Figure F: Option 4: 4 passes to 2 as 1 is slashing down the middle. 2 looks to hit 1 on his cut.

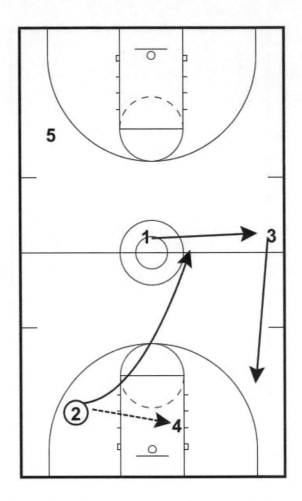

Figure G: If 2 cannot hit 1 on his cut, he reverses to 4 and slashes diagonally, looking for a return pass from 4. 3 cuts to the frontcourt, looking for a pass from 4.

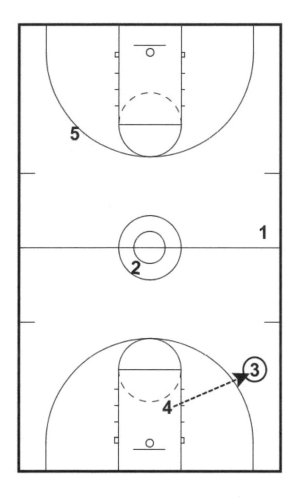

Figure H: 4 passes to 3, who looks for the slasher 2. 4 remains as the reversal target.

Chapter 16: Special Situations — SLOBS and BLOBS

Every game has situations for which teams must be prepared. I believe I have failed as a coach if my team encounters things in a game for which they were not prepared. So almost every practice has a section designated as "special situations" in which we worked on things like out-of-bounds plays, time and score situations, pressing and attacking the press, and any thing else that is unique or out of the ordinary.

There are two places where the ball is taken *out-of-bounds* (OB) and I think that teams must be prepared to inbound the ball from both the baseline (BLOB) and the sideline (SLOB). My teams always had two basic BLOB plays and two SLOB plays. Then as the season progresses, it is good to add variations to these or give them new ones to create interest or to use against certain opponents.

Before you can execute a successful in-bounds play you must have the right player passing the ball inbounds. You shouldn't just let the closest player assume that role. Probably one of the most important things I did in the summer is decide who my throw-in player is to be.

That's so important. He needs to have a clock in his head that ticks off five seconds without him counting. Most players think five seconds is a lot shorter than it is. He needs to know where the ball should go, be able to look away and then come back to his first target. He also needs to know where the ball shouldn't go unless he has no other option.

The *LINE* is the most basic, simple, and useful play we have for an OB situation. I have used it both on the baseline and at the sideline with good success. As the name suggests, there is an in-bounder and four players in a line. I would almost always designate 3 or 4 to throw the ball inbounds and then have 1, 2, 4, (3), and 5 in a vertical line.

On the signal, players 1 and 2 go to opposite corners, player 4 screens for 5 and pops, and player 5 goes off the screen to an open spot. Player 3 then has four options and must be sure to step in-bounds (probably opposite 5).

The second option is "America's Play." Player 1 passes to 4 then down screens for 3 for a shot in the corner.

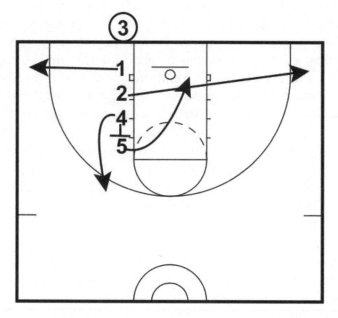

Figure A: We have used the line for both sideline and baseline in-bounds plays. On the signal, 1 and 2 got to opposite corners, 4 screens for 5, then pops to the top. 5 comes off the screen to an open area. The inbounder (3) has four options.

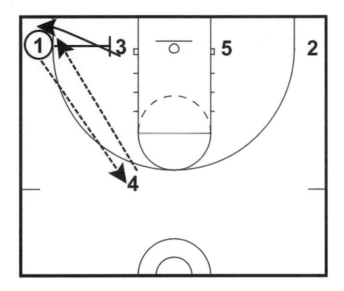

Figure B: After the inbounder (3) steps in at the low block, we are set up for what's come to be known as "America's Inbounds Play" because so many teams use at least a variation of it. Even when an opponent knows what is coming, it often results in a good shot if the execution is good. If the ball goes in the corner to 1, he reverses to 4 and sets a screen for 3 flashing to the corner.

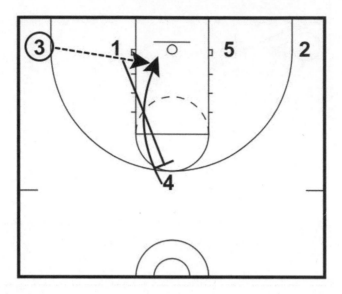

Figure C: Numerous options can be used for this set and teams shouldn't settle for just getting the ball to the corner. For example, after screening to get 3 to the corner, 1 can reverse pivot and set a back screen for 4 after 4 passes to 3 in the corner. Teams that routinely defend every inbounds play with a zone can get caught in their match-up and be vulnerable to this screening action and 4 can get a good shot after cutting down the lane and getting a return pass from 3.

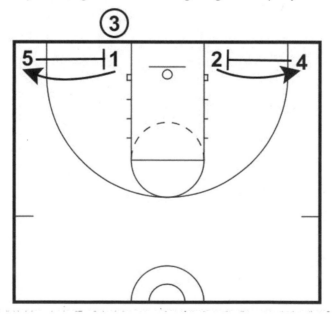

Figure D: We call this inbounds play "Four" simply because we have four players in a line across the baseline. On the signal, 5 and 4 screen for 1 and 2, who each go to the corner.

A second BLOB play is called *FOUR* because we spread four players along the baseline. On the signal, players 5 and 4 down screen for 1 and 2, and 5 keeps going across the lane to screen for 4. Then 5 pivots (opens up) and makes a big target for a pass from 3. Again player 3 has four options and must be sure to step in bounds after his pass. As player 2 becomes the defensive safety, 3 would fill the spot he vacated. A flex cut can be added.

In addition to using LINE as a SLOB, I like to add one more from the sideline, which has good opportunity to score.

In this player, we have player 3 (4) inbound, put 1 and 2 in line with 3, and 4 and 5 are on the block.Player 1 screens for 2 and goes to backcourt. Player 4 screens for 5 and goes to high-

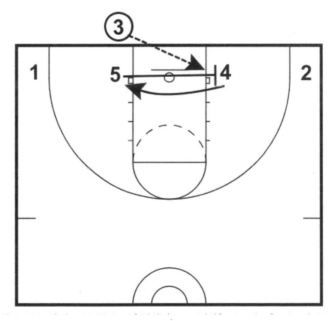

Figure E: 5 continues across the lane to set a screen for 4, who loops over it. After screening, 5 reverse pivots and opens up hard for a pass from 3. It is crucial that the posts be taught to reverse pivot properly; in essence they are blocking out their opponents. This often results in an easy pass for a layup or a lob to 4 on the cut. This alignment forces teams out of playing zone against your inbounds unless they are willing to give up and uncontested pass to the corner. After the block-to-block screen is set, 2 must fire up to the top to act as the "safety" defender. Once the ball is inbounded, teams can add a flex cut as a secondary option.

post.Player 2 comes off the screen to receive the ball and 5 comes off the screen to back-screen for 3. If done correctly, the ball would go from 3 to 2, from 2 to 4, and from 4 to 3 for an easy shot. If nothing is open, pass to 1 in backcourt and begin the offense.

I wish I had a nickel for every time I've stood up on the sidelines and said "Time and Score." I wanted our team to score as time ran out — to get the last shot of the quarter and not give our opponent enough time to score. Typically that meant with less than 25 seconds left in a quarter, hold the ball until the clock is down to 8 seconds and then run something special and score at 3 seconds.

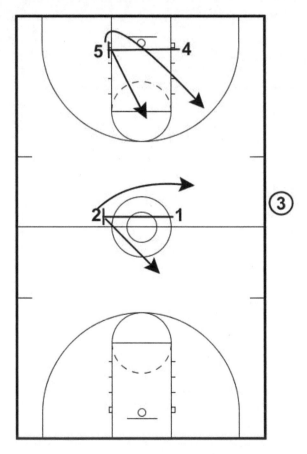

Figure F: 3 is our inbounder with 1 and 2 in line with the ball and 4 and 5 on the blocks. 1 screens for 2, then opens up to the backcourt as a safety valve. 2 loops over and calls for the ball. 4 screens for 5 and breaks to just above the free throw line.

Here's how I wanted these last seconds to go — the clock is under 30 seconds in the first, second, or third quarter. I would stand up and say loudly "Time and Score." The players knew to take care of the ball, hold the ball as they ran some offense like wheel or flex. At eight seconds, I (or the point guard) would say "go," which meant we would run a special The special could mean a staggered screen to give a good three-point to our shooter, or a dribble drive or flex for a good shot.

We didn't want "time and score" to give our opponents an advantage, so a reminder about crashing the boards was stressed in practice – we just sent one player to the boards while the other players were in defensive transition.

We didn't always score, but at least our opponent didn't have enough time to score.

Other situations that fall in the category of Time and Score are:

- Last 2 minutes of game, down 3 points

- Last 1 minute of game, up by 4 points

- Last 10 seconds

- Last 4 seconds

- And many more.

Each of these Special Situations must be practiced several times a week so that our team is prepared to carry out our game plan. You cannot neglect the preparations for these.

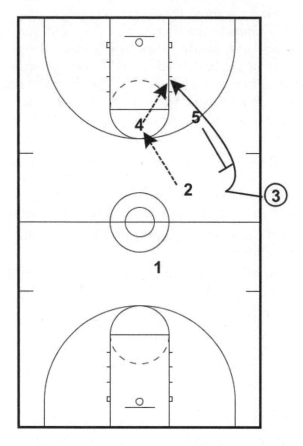

Figure G: 5 comes off the screen to set a back screen or 3, who jab-steps when he steps in bounds to set up his man for the screen. If executed properly, the ball is passed from 2 to 4, who pivots and looks for 3 coming off the screen and going to the basket. If the play breaks down, 1 hustles to the front court to take a pass from 4 and set up the offense.

Chapter 17:
Time Out for a Few Thoughts About Timeouts

Timeouts are a strategic aspect of games and the successful coach will learn to manage them. A coach has no more than 60 seconds — sometimes only half that — to get his players focused, to tell them what adjustments they need to make and to make sure they understand how they were instructed by the coach.

High school basketball allows five timeouts per game: three are for 60 seconds and two for 30 seconds. Some people believe a coach is really coaching if he uses all five timeouts. In looking back at my career I believe I did not use all of my timeouts in most of our games — but there are times when I would have liked to have more. Sometimes I called one because we just needed a break, other times to halt an opponent's surge. Most often I used them to change strategy and sometimes to stop the clock late in the game.

In a competitive game I will use one early in the game if things aren't going well or if our opponent is doing something we weren't prepared for. A good time to call one if things are going well is with five minutes left in the first half. By then, we have made some substitutions, the players are into the rhythm of the game and we can talk about finishing strong until halftime.

I always preferred to have four timeouts left for the second half and at least three for the fourth quarter. The fourth period has so many times when:

- Your opponent is making a run

- You want to stop the clock

- You want to emphasize something

- You want to hold the ball for the last shot

If possession of the ball is gained with the score tied or you are down 1-3 points with limited time, my philosophy is NOT to call a timeout. I have tried to coach players to make good choices and so I would probably let them play and show they have been coached well enough to have them make their own decisions.

If we are holding the ball for the last shot I would probably call a timeout with 14 seconds left to make sure we are all on the same page about how we are going to play it—probably a set play for your best player that results in a good shot with three seconds left on the clock.

It has become very popular to call timeouts to avoid a turnover, when there is a scramble for the ball on the floor or when the ball is going out of bounds. That can be acceptable in the fourth quarter, but I don't encourage those kinds of "possession timeouts" early in the game. At that point I believe we could better lose a possession rather than lose a timeout.

A coach must use timeouts (and time between quarters) to make changes in personnel and strategy, and be able to make game adjustments. However, I don't believe in calling timeout when we are 12 points down with a minute left to play. Be kind to the people in the stands; there are no seven-point plays in basketball.

Players should not be allowed to call timeouts on their own. I had a player call a timeout once because things weren't going his way. Another time a player called a timeout when we had no timeouts left.

During timeouts I want the five players in the game to sit directly in front of me. A player who just came out of the game should move to the background and give input only if asked. The head coach needs to communicate to the players who are in the game and the others must know to move back. The same goes for assistant coaches: seek their input before you talk to the players. It is counter-productive if the assistant coaches are talking to each other or to the players while I am talking to the five who are in the game.

Every coach must realize that some players don't hear instructions if they only hear it once. Before they go back on the floor I would ask them to repeat to me what I said to them. A team can't have four players in a zone and one player in a man-to-man. It's not good enough that the players listen to me. They must hear me — and they must understand what I told them.

Chapter 18: From My Driveway to the Championship

I coached 48 different varsity basketball teams at Denver Christian. Each of them was a unique mix of players, strengths and weaknesses. I've always shied away from labeling one team as my "favorite," but I have to confess a special fondness for the one that germinated in my driveway.

Greg Ham, an honor student and point guard, lived a few blocks away. Greg Nyhoff, who would grow into a steady and versatile inside presence, lived across the alley from me. Their friend and teammate was my son, Keith, whose downstairs room was a frequent gathering place for the neighborhood boys.

From the time they were seventh graders, this trio and several of their classmates would play "around the world" and two-on-two games for endless hours in our driveway and talk about how they were going to win a state championship when they were seniors in 1978.

If I heard "**State in '78**" once, I heard it a thousand times.

In those days, Denver Christian was primarily a neighborhood/church school. I think the feeling was not unlike growing up in a small town where everyone gravitated to the school on game nights.

Said Ham of that time, "We didn't just know him as a coach; he was my friend's dad. He would carpool us to school and home after practice in a green Chevy with big tail fins. What I remember from when I was very young is that he always seemed to have a smile on his face and was pretty happy. He taught me a lot about what it was like to be a man, a man of God first and foremost."

"He integrated his faith in God and Christ into everything he did. We saw him in church every Sunday. That faith in God

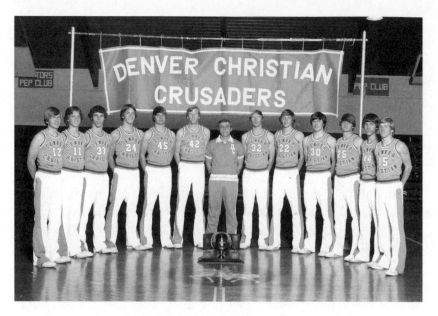

From left to right, Ed Buteyn, Russ Smith, Keith Katte, Craig Matthies, Greg Lucht, Eric Forseth, Coach Katte, Greg Nyhoff, Colin Barr, Jim Dumler, Steve Wolffis, Lee Poulette, Greg Ham (Photo by Zemi Photographics)

was the biggest thing he taught us and it has helped me throughout my life."

"As youngsters whenever there was a game on Friday or Saturday night we'd all pile in the car and go. We idolized those varsity players. Our junior high teams were good, and we didn't lose a game when we were freshmen."

It wasn't just basketball. These boys were real friends, and it was great having them hang around our house, even though they probably put a dent in our food budget for a few years. They really loved Lorraine's cooking and baking.

Nyhoff remembers, "Dick and Lorraine were great with us. It wasn't like he was running around telling everybody what to do all the time. The thing about Dick was he didn't have to yell at you to motivate you. You just wanted to give everything every single minute you were on the court. We were the kind of team that was going to lay it out every single time and it was because of him."

"He never demanded your respect, he just earned it very naturally. You always knew he was thinking about you, saying 'How's school going?' or 'How's it going with your girlfriend?'.

"I attribute a lot of what I am today to him. Every human being has importance. I was a role player that he appreciated. He stressed not letting anybody in the middle score without a battle from me, and I knew I mattered just as much to him as the guys who scored 20 points a game. I didn't realize all the things I learned from him that carried on as I grew up. Life is one competitive whirl, and he always had a strategy for each situation. Today I'm a city manager (in Modesto, Calif.,) and we have to figure out things like how to fight crime better."

If the team had been formed with the kids in that class it would have been a very strong team, maybe good enough to win a championship, but a couple of very important pieces showed up to complete the puzzle and make the dream come true.

When Denver Chrsitian expanded its mission to all Christian families rather than being a school just for children of the Christian Reformed Church, it provided even more teachable moments for us.

DC had been a school where most of the students were from Christian homes and their Christianity was assumed. In the 1970s we began enrolling Christian students from different backgrounds. Some families came in needing a more structured environment than they received from their previous schools.

Eric Forseth went to Hamilton Junior High School in Denver, and everyone thought he was destined for big-school stardom along with his then-classmates Michael Smith and David Black at Thomas Jefferson High School, a longtime Denver prep power. Instead, Eric's family steered him to Denver Christian, where he became a starter as a sophomore on our 1976 state runner-up team.

Eric's mother was diagnosed with multiple sclerosis when he was six years old. She had just delivered twins, and the doctors wouldn't allow her to hold them for fear she would drop them. Mrs. Forseth spent much of Eric's formative years in a wheelchair. They had our family over for dinner, and I was so impressed with the loving way each of them treated and cared for her. Each one of the children had special duties for their mom, which they carried out so beautifully.

"That kind of thing shapes your life," said Forseth, who was a vice president at his college alma mater, Northwest Nazarene University, before becoming the superintendent of Nampa Christian Schools in Nampa, Idaho and is currently provost at Dordt College in Sioux Center, Iowa. "I think it made me more determined, more focused, more intense about seizing opportunities."

The final piece was a sophomore, Craig Matthies, who was well on his way to becoming the most prolific scorer in Denver Christian history.

"He was quiet, unassuming and loved the game; lived and died to play the game," Ham recalls of Matthies, who had been the Crusaders' sixth man and the first freshman every to play varsity for Katte. "I don't think any of the older players resented a young sophomore scoring a lot of points. We all just enjoyed the success we were having so much and Craig did a great job of putting the ball in the hole."

There is a difference between being a shooter and a scorer, but Craig Matthies was both. He could hit midrange-plus jump shots as well as get to the basket with moves the Denver Post called "unbelievable." It was in the interview for that story that he also learned a valuable lesson after telling reporter Michael Knisley that if Christian was going to lose it probably wouldn't be until the state tournament. When you encourage teenage boys to talk to the media, you have to live with the good and the bad.

"Coach let me know that we only talk about the next game and I didn't make that mistake again," said Matthies.

"I remember a lot of times our practices were harder than the games," said Matthies. "He was the kind of coach that if he told you to run into a wall, that's what you did. You could never cross him. We did hit heads a few times because I was a scorer first and foremost, and he might have had a hard time with that. That senior group was so intense and so competitive. Eric and I would really go at it. Winning state was always

our goal. By midseason we expected to win it, but we knew it wouldn't be wise to say it."

Greg Lucht, whose father was the principal and head basketball coach at Christian when my career began, came off the bench and played in every game, as did hard-nosed defender Steve Wolffis.

"I remember as you put me into the game, you put your arm around me and told me, 'Do what you do well. Push those big guys out of there and get those rebounds.' Those words have come to mind throughout my life and given me strength in challenging times. Simple and clear words of instruction to get the job done," said Lucht.

I knew we'd be able to score and that Forseth and Nyhoff would control the boards but I put a great deal of emphasis on teamwork, taking pride in their passing, and good defense. The talent on that team was deep enough that Matthies and a core of non-starters on the team were state runner-up a year later and won a state championship of their own two years later.

Just before the season started, Ham found himself in Katte's disciplinary sights. The coach stressed to the team not to forget to bring their uniforms to school for picture day.

"Of course I forgot mine and had to call my mom to bring it up to me," said Ham. Normally, that kind of infraction would result in pre-practice running until a heaving chest and rubber legs would emphasize the importance of not repeating the error.

This time, however, the I meted out a more cerebral — and time-consuming — regimen.

"He told me my punishment was to go home and read the Book of Proverbs," recalled Ham.

"At the time I was a little ticked off, but there was a lot of core wisdom scripture about what it means to meet responsibility, not be lazy and be on time. I came back and told him what I had learned from that. That was kind of a unique Dick Katte approach and obviously I still remember it. I think it was less about me forgetting my uniform than it was that he thought I was a little too full of myself at that time in my life, that I needed to slow down and think about what was important."

The biggest setback for the team and for me personally occurred two months before the season began. My son Keith was an outstanding football player, one of the best running backs in the state and had started for Christian since he was a sophomore. We were playing at Limon and he was running a sweep on the first play of the second quarter. It was third down and as Keith leaned for an extra yard, one defender had him by the leg and another one hit him and twisted it. Both the anterior and medial collateral ligaments were torn.

This was before reconstructive surgery was common, especially for high school players. He wore an ankle-to-thigh cast for six weeks but when he began to rehabilitate and run, he noticed a catch in the knee whenever he tried to cut. A trip to the orthopedic surgeon confirmed cartilage damage and a subsequent operation revealed the ligament tears.

"I elected not to have something major done," said Keith. "My parents left it up to me. They knew how important it was that we had set out with a mission, a goal to win that state championship. Every day in practice I'd get it taped up to hold it as best it could but if I planted my left foot and tried to push off, I'd be down in a heap on the floor. That was part of what I made a choice to deal with."

Watching a player try to fight through an injury is tough enough, but when it's your own son it's doubly difficult.

"When Keith would land wrong on that knee and go down in a heap, you could see how Dick's heart was going out to him, but he didn't baby him either. It was tough for both of them to deal with that adversity. A coach would feel bad for any player in that situation but when it's your son it had to be doubly difficult," said Ham.

The injury robbed Keith of some of his quickness. He became more of an outside shooter, but his positional defense, a topic of basketball conversation in his house as long as he could remember, remained a constant.

This is a good time to deal with an issue many coaches have to face: coaching your own son. There is no doubt it can be a difficult situation but it can also be a wonderful experience for both the parent and the child.

It's an old joke in the coaching profession that, "I'm going to start my best four players and my son." That wasn't an issue with us because everyone knew Keith was one of our five best players, even after the injury, and everyone had tremendous respect for the way their friend endured all of that pain so he could be part of the team.

I think most of the problems in a coach/son relationship come when one of them has unrealistic expectations about his role on the team. If a coach plays his own son ahead of more talented players, there is going to be a lot of resentment. It can turn the players against both the coach and his son. On the other hand, if a coach is harsher on his child than he is on the rest of the team, it can strain the relationship within your family — which is a lot more important than anything that happens on the basketball floor. I think both of us knew it wouldn't be easy but we both cherish these moments today.

In our case I think Keith probably felt a little more pressure than I did.

"Growing up and knowing his philosophy and talking at home, I knew exactly what was expected," Keith said. "I knew and he knew that it wasn't the kind of thing where I had to be as good as the other guy, I had to be better if I was going to earn a starting position.

"It was a conscious thing I was aware of and there was some additional pressure on and off the court. Whatever I did he was going to know about it, and I probably toed the line a little more than some of the others just because of that respect. I didn't want to let him down, didn't want to bring anything to light that would reflect negatively on him as a parent. It was also very rewarding and fun to be part of that and to experience it like we did and come home and talk about things in a strategic kind of way."

We began the season ranked fourth in the state and opened against then-top ranked Lewis Palmer, which had bumped us from the playoffs a year earlier. We won 60-47, and the victory vaulted us to the top spot in the polls. Next game was at Highland of Ault.

It was a close game, and in the third quarter, Eric Forseth, who had already scored 20 points, decided to help the referee make a call and was whistled for a technical foul. The foul meant he was done for the game—that was my rule. When Craig Matthies fouled out in the fourth quarter, I turned to my assistant, and asked "Think we should put Forseth back in?" That would break our unwritten rule that a player who got a technical had to sit the rest of the game. We decided that we weren't going to compromise our principles, and he needed to know the consequences of getting that technical. We didn't put him back in and the other guys stepped up and we won 62-56.

"That was just one of many what I would call 'redirections' by Dick Katte," recalled Forseth. "He told me, 'that's not a demonstration of character." The message stuck for a lifetime. "I'm a provost today because I wanted to be like him as a teacher, an educator and an administrator. I'm a positive person today because of his influence yesterday. I've always said that the reality of Dick Katte was bigger than the legend. I often find myself thinking, 'What would he do?' in some situation. He has great intuition. He always knows what to say and what not to say."

The Crusaders cruised through the season. The only close call we had was a 62-60 victory over Summit in the Metro League tournament championship. We lost Eric Forseth and Craig Matthies to fouls and made a lot of bad turnovers and forced shots in the fourth quarter, but in the end, Greg Ham hit a free throw in the final 10 seconds to put us up by two. Then Steve Wolffis controlled a jump ball in the final seconds.

Some people think it's best to lose a game along the way so your players won't feel the pressure of being undefeated, but I disagree. I've never really believed in losing a game just for the sake of losing. I don't ever want to lose. My idea is to expose them to failure in practice by making things as difficult as we could. I don't think a loss would have motivated that team any more than they already were. From seventh grade on they had that driving goal to win state.

Even more than most years, I felt I needed to challenge this team by scrimmaging against the best teams in the state.

Back then you didn't have as many restrictions on scrimmages, and we always tried to find the best teams in 3A (then the largest classification) to practice against. We went up against George Washington, Manual and all the good suburban teams. I think that kept us sharp and ready to play against the best teams in 2A.

We all got a good lesson when we went up against Green Mountain.

"They beat us pretty soundly," recalled Nyhoff. "Coach said, 'Don't ever think there's not a team out there that can't beat you if you don't play your game.'"

We had a tough first-round matchup at state against a Platte Valley team that was 19-2 and led us 29-25 at halftime. Matthies caught fire and finished with 29 points and 12 rebounds, and we switched to our 1-3-1 in the second half and wound up winning 63-57. We were in the state semifinals, but neither the players nor the coaches were happy with the way we had played in the last two games.

"At one point in the second half, coach turned to me and said, 'you're just not here, Nyhoff. What's the story?' I thought I was playing hard but I realized I wasn't giving as much as I could.

"We got home late that night and the team met without the coaches after returning to school. We decided, 'We have to let this go. We can't be hesitant or tentative. Are we really as good as we think we are?'"

Turns out they were. We bounced back with a 67-36 victory over Gunnison in the semifinals to get to the championship game against Highland, which hadn't lost since we had beaten them in the second game of the season.

Highland had a great player named Jim Turner who had scored 60 points in the first two tournament games, so I assigned Keith to guard him straight up while the rest of the team played a four-man zone.

"We had run that diamond-and-one a few times throughout the year, and I was the chaser who had the assignment to stop their shooter. When I needed a break, Steve Wolffis came in and played that role," recalled Keith.

We held Highland to 16 of 73 shooting and went on a 19-point run starting late in the second quarter and wound up winning 62-42. All 12 players on the roster got into the box score.

When the game was over I felt like I needed to talk to Jim Turner who finished with 10 points. I put my arm around him and told him I was sorry to have to employ a gimmick defense against him, but that that it had been our team's best chance to win. I hope he took that as a compliment.

Forseth, Matthies and Keith were selected all-tournament. Forseth and Matthies made every all-state team; Forseth was Colorado Sidelines' AA Player of the Year and was second-team (along with his junior high teammate Black) on The Denver Post's all-classification honor team. Black and Forseth were pictured side-by-side on the Rocky Mountain News' all-Metro Denver team, which was ironic given that they could have wound up on the same high school team.

"What I remembered most about that year is that we'd all be at each other's houses all the time. It was the most selfless group of individuals I've ever experienced in my lifetime. It was a true team. It didn't matter who scored, who passed, who rebounded," said Ham.

Keith Katte recalled the team joking that there would never be enough basketballs on the floor to suit Forseth and Matthies, "But it was OK that they were scoring most of the points. It was never about any one of us. We recognized that and played together."

Our winning streak stretched through the first seven games of the next season before Holy Family gave us our only loss during the regular season. Glenwood Springs beat us for the state championship.

That championship team started a run that put Denver Christian basketball on the map at the state level. We went 131-18 over the next six seasons and won four state championships, including a back-to-back in 1982 and 1983.

Chapter 19: A Great Run to Another Title

The class of 1980 was the team in waiting. They turned out to be worth waiting for.

Two years earlier, Craig Matthies was the leading scorer on our undefeated team. Many of his classmates were reserves on that team, and their role was to push the starters hard in practice.

A year later they came together as a group and became a formidable team, winning a fourth consecutive Metro League championship. It didn't come easily or without personal cost to one of them.

Harold Pranger, a 6'6" junior, was projected to be our dominant inside player. In our third game he went up for a rebound, and his leg snapped in the air. When he landed, the leg folded, bones protruding. I don't remember ever seeing a more shocking sight in my career. He was taken away in an ambulance, and we finished the game in a very subdued fashion. Harold had surgery and spent time rehabilitating, but he was injured again during the summer.

Keith Aardema and Larry Rosendale stepped up for Harold in our inside game. We ran our winning streak to 32 games, lost to Holy Family in the final seconds, then won 16 in a row before losing in the state championship game to a quick, big and savvy Glenwood Springs team.

That loss made the team even more determined — and they were a pretty determined group even before that. They were fun to coach because they had a true love for the game in addition to being the best offensive team in school history. They averaged 78 points a game and shot better than 48 percent from the field. Twice we scored 100 points, including a 115-

1980 Champions: Kent Hamstra, Russ Smith, Don VanZytveld, Paul Trollinger, Ron Forseth, Larry Rosendale, Jeff Van Kooten, Craig Matthies, Colin Barr, Harvey Brasser, Brad LeFebre, Greg VanderMeulen (Photo by Zemi Photographics)

point performance against Sheridan — in which every player on the roster scored at least six points — that still stands as a Crusader single game scoring record.

Matthies was a superb offensive talent who could get off his shot against anyone, including the variety of gimmick defenses he faced that year. It wasn't his best scoring year (18.1 points), but so many of our regular season games were blowouts that he didn't get a lot of playing time in the fourth quarter. As it was, he finished his four-year varsity career as the leading scorer in Crusader history with 1,746 points. Until recently he ranked among the top 10 scorers in state history.

Russ Smith was the perfect point guard for that team. He pushed the pace, shot just enough to keep defenses honest and had nearly twice as many assists as anyone else on the team. He controlled us on offense and on defense because he could cover two guys from the top of our 1-3-1. A coach doesn't realize how important an outstanding point guard is until he doesn't have one, and Russ certainly made my job easier.

Russ had been waiting for this opportunity since he was a youngster. He had attended DC games with his grandfather, who took tickets at the door.

"I would sit in the front row and watch, looking forward to one day, playing for Coach Katte, in that gym, representing the Crusader basketball program. I would go home after games and make jerseys out of old t-shirts, writing 'Crusaders' on the front and the number of my favorite player at the time on the back. My dad put a hoop in my basement and I would play hours down there, pretending to be on the team," he said.

Larry Rosendale, who was 6'6", gave us a strong inside presence and was our second-leading scorer and rebounder (behind Craig). Colin Barr was the perfect companion beside Matthies: a slasher to the basket and a good passer who was also our student body president. Paul Trollinger, who started at the off-guard, was a good fit with that unit: a good defender who didn't need to shoot a lot and took care of the ball. We had nine seniors on that team, which was a lot, even for a program like ours that tried to keep as many seniors as we could. (The other seniors were Harvey Brasser, Brad LeFebre, Greg Vander Meulen, Don Van Zytveld; and juniors: Ron Forseth, Kent Hamstra and Jeff Van Kooten.)

I encourage players to play other sports, but we didn't have many multi-sport players on that team. Some of them played soccer or track, but they were mainly basketball players.

We started the season with seven consecutive victories and were ranked in the top spot until we ran into our rival Holy Family — and yet another Golesh boy.

We had a 36-game home winning streak on that December night, but Holy Family took us to overtime and came away with a 64-59 victory. Pete Golesh, a junior, scored 19 points for the Tigers (four of them in overtime).

Michael Knisley of *The Denver Post* wrote an entertaining and well-researched column the next week about the basketball history between the Golesh family and Denver Christian.

Pete was the fourth of six Golesh boys, and every one of them saved some of their best performances for games against Denver Christian! Matt had 18 points when Holy Family beat us for the state championship in 1976 after we had defeated them three times that season. Ned hit a buzzer-beater from 20 feet to nip us by a point and break our 32-game winning streak in 1979.

I told Michael Kinsley at the time that the Golesh boys were fierce competitors, "but when they're done, they're class people."

We were able to return the favor to Holy Family in our second meeting, another overtime thriller in their gym. Craig Matthies had 27 points and 13 rebounds, and he and Russ Smith both hit big free throws for us in the final couple of minutes after Pete Golesh tied the score for the last time in regulation.

We advanced to the Metro League tournament championship and defeated Holy Family again (70-66) and were playing well heading into the state playoffs. Of course our players' goal was to win state, but we kept that low-key. I reminded them, "Don't miss the season because of focusing on the destination."

Despite our success, there were a few rough spots in the season. Our student support has always been excellent. However, about a month before the playoffs, we had to admonish them for some unsportsmanlike behavior, especially against our biggest rivals. And it wasn't just the students. Some of our adult fans were also doing some things that didn't reflect a positive image on our school and our community. As I said at the time, "Booing and yelling should not be part of our image. Others do judge us on our Christian character, and the behavior of the parents has not been very positive in some cases. We cannot have a double standard—expecting the students to be good sports when the adults aren't."

Going into the tournament, *the Post's* Mike Monroe proclaimed us as the "team to beat," despite Lewis-Palmer being undefeated and led by a great player—Scott Mann, a 6'6" senior who had 33 points, 26 rebounds and 8 assists in their district playoff victory.

We defeated Olathe to get to the semifinals against Yuma, coached by Ken Shaw, who was not only one of the most prolific scorers in Colorado prep history but also coached different teams to five state championships. We had a history together since I had coached him in the All-State game 10 years earlier.

A year earlier we came back from four points down in the last minute to defeat Yuma in the quarterfinals and this year's game was just as tight. We trailed by eight points going into the fourth quarter and were behind 55-52 with 45 seconds left. Russ Smith hit two free throws to get us within a point. They missed a free throw with 17 seconds left and Craig Matthies got the rebound.

Craig scored 18 points in the first half but had struggled with his shot and with foul trouble in the second. Larry Rosendale got him the ball as he was cutting to the basket, and he scored to give us the lead with five seconds left. Yuma called timeout, but they turned the ball over and we were on our way to the championship game.

It was a classic match up of the top two ranked teams. Lewis Palmer was undefeated; we had only that overtime loss to Holy Family.

Our first half was almost flawless offensively. We pushed the ball hard, and when I went to the bench, Ron Forseth, Jeff Van Kooten and Brad LeFebre didn't lose a step from our starters, and we went into halftime with a 43-26 lead. Defensively, our 1-3-1 kept them off balance.

To their credit, Lewis-Palmer came back and cut our lead to 10 points with a little less than six minutes to play, but, having learned the lesson of not sitting on a lead, we kept the offensive pressure on and pulled away for a 76-60 victory and our third state championship. It culminated an amazing run of two state championships and a 72-3 record over three seasons.

Our captains—Craig, Russ and Colin—each had two of those championships as well as a second-place finish. They took charge from the beginning and accounted for every one of our 18 points in the first quarter. Craig finished with 19 points, Colin had 16 and Russ more than doubled his season average with 14. All three of them made the all-tournament team.

"Coach Katte was our leader, but he was also interested in having relationships with his players," said Smith. " I can remember him sitting with us by our lockers, talking about school, family, girls... life. That was important. He also allowed his other coaches to build relationships and use their

183

*gifts to build the program. Coach Van was also very signifi-
cant to me (and our teams) and my success as a player for
DC."*

Any question about Craig's ability to play at the highest
level was answered when he was the only small-school player
chosen for a Colorado All-Star team to play in the Cerebral
Palsy-McDonald's High School All-Star Basketball Classic in
Salt Lake City. He earned a scholarship to Biola University, a
Christian college in southern California, but a back injury cur-
tailed his college career.

Mann, who was honorable mention all-WAC player as a a
senior at Colorado State, finished with 19 points and set a
class AA state tournament record with 28 rebounds, but Larry
Rosendale made him work for every one of those points. Over
the years, I have run into Scott Mann when his sons were playing high school basketball.

With a team is as talented as this one, I tried to remind them
to be sure that the season gave them some "Forever Moments"—lasting memories rather than only instant glory. Even
more than our season's success on the court, I wanted them to
take the season's journey with them.

I was gratified at the "after basketball" careers of these men.
Two of them played small-college basketball; two became teachers after realizing that the business world was not giving them
fulfillment. Three others became very successful in the business world. Five of them had sons I wound up coaching in
later years. Russ Smith still teaches at Denver Christian Middle
School and was an assistant coach in our program for ten years.

Chapter 20: From Underdogs to Champions — Twice

I don't have an exact count but after 52 years on the bench, I'm guessing that I coached 12 varsity players each year. On average six of those would have been seniors, so my total number of players coached comes out a little north of 300.

I've been fortunate to have many players who have been selected all-state, tournament MVPs and all-conference.

But of them all, one stands out: Jim De Groot was without a doubt the best player I ever coached. During my coaching tenure, I developed a pretty good eye for spotting potential players, but the first time I saw Jim De Groot I never would have pegged him as the best player I would ever coach.

He was a 5'10" junior who had transferred into Denver Christian in the fall of 1980 and wasn't eligible to play with us until mid-season. Jim had grown up in California and was a varsity player as a sophomore at Saddleback High School in Santa Ana. His father was a land surveyor and joined the company that was developing Highlands Ranch. The family moved to Colorado after Jim's basketball season was over.

Jim remembers, "My first night in Denver, dad said, 'Let's watch the state finals on TV.' It was the year Denver Christian won it when Craig Matthies was a senior. I knew in my heart I wanted to go there but I wound up finishing my sophomore year at Smoky Hill. It didn't work out at all. My parents knew I was unhappy. We're Dutch. I'd grown up in Christian schools through eighth grade, and they knew I wanted to go to Denver Christian. I was back in my element, from the teachers to the students, even to being small."

When he became eligible (after sitting out a semester following his transfer), he made us a lot better. However, he was very undisciplined. That year we were 17-4, lost in the first

1982 Champions: Back row from left, Randy Van Roekel, Greg LeFebre, Greg Baltzer, Coach Katte, Roger Navis, Craig Kispert, Mark Spinder. Front row from left, Greg Ruter, Bob Engelsman, Todd Schneider, Jim DeGroot, Steve Thomas, Daryl Van Kooten (Photo by Zemi Photographics)

round of the state tournament and came back for the consolation title.

I watched him play against Division I players at DU during the summers, and he more than held his own. He was a great, pure talent. He could always play defense and protect the ball, and by the time he was a senior he'd learned to shoot. That was the difference between being a pretty good player and a great one.

Jim says, "My shot was flat, kind of a knuckleball. Coach Katte brought in Roger Morningstar who played at Kansas for his summer camp and all of a sudden it clicked for me. He talked about the arch and how two balls could fit inside the basket. When school started the next year some of my friends wanted me to play football, but I went to the YMCA every day and worked really hard on my shot," he said.

Not only did he work hard on his shot that summer, Jim grew three inches between his junior and senior year. So I decided he would play point guard on offense and center in our zone on defense.

Jim says, "To Coach Katte's credit, he could have just stuck me at guard and small forward, but he was creative and open minded enough to move me around. I was long and had learned to block shots with my left hand because you're not reaching across your body and fouling. It was a really good fit for what we had going on."

Jim's senior season statistical line was amazing: He led us in scoring (17.1), rebounding (7.0), steals (4.2), blocked shots (3.8), shot 52 percent from the field and 75 percent from the free throw line. Perhaps most impressive was the fact that he had nearly as many assists (114) as the rest of the team combined (135), and he made everyone on the team a better player.

That '81-'82 team was a mix of youth and experience. Only De Groot had seen much time the previous year, but sophomores Craig Kispert (6'3") and Greg Balltzer (6'3") had the potential and experience to step right in. Greg Le Febre (6'4") provided a good inside presence for a junior, and senior guard Randy Van Roekel was anxious to have his turn. Others (Bob Engelsman, Roger Navis, Greg Ruter, Todd Schneider, Mark Spinder, Steve Thomas and Daryl Van Kooten) were on the roster that developed into a formidable team.

We began the season ranked second in the state, but lost two of our first three games (to Mapleton and Bishop Machebeuf). After that we ran off 16 in a row. One of the games in that streak, when we beat Machebeuf 70-63 in a return match, was a classic match-up that I always remember fondly.

DeGroot scored 34 points, and Machebeuf's Dick Pennefather scored 36. We couldn't stop Pennefather, and they couldn't stop DeGroot. I'm not sure I ever saw anyone shoot as well as Pennefather did that night.

By the way, if the Pennefather name rings a bell, it's probably because of Dick's sister, Shelly. She was generally acknowledged as the best female player in Colorado high school history. She never lost a game in high school (96-0 in three years at Machebeuf and her senior year in New York where she moved with her family). She was a three-time Big East Player of the Year at Villanova. Her record of 2,408 points has never been broken by any Villanova athlete, male or female, and she won the Margaret Wade trophy emblematic of the nation's best female player.

After earning $100,000 a season playing professionally in Japan, she stepped away from the secular world. In 1991 she became a cloistered nun, Sister Rose Marie of the Order of Poor Clares.

I admire someone who has the ability, the opportunity for glamour, for high profile, but because of a commitment — in her case a religious commitment, a calling — she put all that aside because she wanted to serve God and the Catholic church. I can't say enough positive things about a person who has that kind of character. She completely withdrew from all the acclaim for herself because of her beliefs.

Returning to Jim DeGroot's senior year, Holy Family upset us in a sub district game that I didn't think we should have lost. I called Jim into my office for a chat.

Jim remembers, "It wasn't a long conversation. He said, 'It's go time, Jim.' I was basically bored. I'd lost my passion for playing because sometimes it was too easy. Whatever he said was something to the effect that it was time to get focused. He didn't talk about winning but more of a John Wooden thing of 'Let's get out there and do our best'."

That loss to Holy Family meant we had to take a seven-hour, 321-mile trip in a pair of vans to Ignacio, on the Southern Ute Indian Reservation in southwest Colorado.

"We hadn't pressed much that season but coach decided to press that evening to create some energy and it stoked me," said De Groot.

We did everything together for three days: we practiced at Adams State and shared a lot of things together. When we won the game 67-53 we got back in the vans, and arrived back in Denver at 7 a.m. I'm sure of the time, because I was driving one of the vans.

Denver Christian was certainly not the favorite when we got to state, but our team saved their best for the biggest stage.

1983 CLASS AA
STATE CHAMPIONS

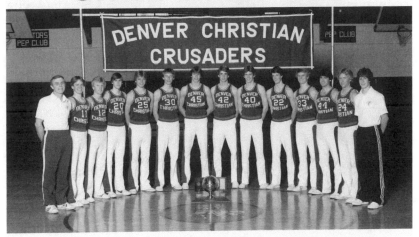

Left to Right: Coach Dick Katte, Tim Spykstra, Steve Thomas, Greg Ruter, Karl Kaemingk, Jay Forseth, Greg LeFebre, Craig Kispert, Greg Baltzer, Dave Medema, Todd Schneider, Bob Engelsman, Guy Boyer, Manager Rich Cok.

Photo by Zemi Photographics

Against favored Nucla (20-1) and the state's leading scorer Ted Davis (25 per game) in the first round, we forced 28 turnovers, which is the most I can ever remember us causing. De Groot had 30 points, 13 rebounds and six assists in an 86-58 victory.

The next night Jim scored 27 points including 15 in a row in our 69-53 victory over University in the semifinals to put us in the championship game against Florence, which was undefeated and ranked first in the state.

Jim says, "I played my best basketball those two previous games. I even had half a dunk. I went up to slam it but it hit the front of the rim, bounced off the backboard and went in. But by the championship game I was just beat, tired. My legs just weren't there."

I'm sure a lot of people thought we were a one-man team, but we had become a solid, deep group. The other players knew we needed Jim to take a lot of shots, but we had plenty of players who were capable of stepping up.

Jim limped throughout that final game, and Florence wisely overplayed him but Randy VanRoekel's outside shooting, and Craig Kispert and Greg LeFebre's inside work kept us within a point going into the fourth quarter at McNichols Sports Arena, the precursor of today's Pepsi Center in downtown Denver.

Their top two scorers had taken 20 shots between them in the first half, so I switched to a triangle-and-two at halftime which slowed them down a little. De Groot missed five of his first seven shots and was limited to 14 points, but contributed seven assists and 13 rebounds.

With the game on the line, Jim dished to Greg for what turned into a three-point play, hit a driving layup that gave us a four-point lead and then converted an off-balance tip-in for our final points

"Randy is the reason we won the championship," said De Groot. "He hit some big outside shots and Greg was just a beast inside."

Florence coach John Merriam was a model of graciousness in defeat. He told the Pueblo Chieftan's *Dave Socier: "We've been fortunate all year. We've been able to play our (fast breaking) game. They took us out of it."*

Jim was the state tournament's Most Valuable Player, a consensus All-State selection, and the only small-school player chosen to the Denver Post's all-Metro team.

What a lot of people don't know about that season is that our most inspirational team member was our scorekeeper.

Jim Greenfield was a talented junior guard who had been penciled in as a likely starter next to DeGroot. He injured his knee during the summer and underwent arthroscopic surgery to remove some stray cartilage that hampered his mobility. Something went wrong. An artery was cut and he faced two more surgeries to save his leg.

With his dream of playing dashed for at least a year, Jim kept our scorebook and watched the players who would have been his teammates celebrate a state championship.

Jim's parents had moved to Brighton, CO from Chicago. Jim went to a Lutheran grade school there, and everybody expected him to go to Lutheran High School. But he started coming to our games and just liked the way we played. His dad brought him down from Brighton every day—a trip of about 30 miles one way.

There was no doubt he would have been a leader of our team if he hadn't become hurt. His life wasn't in jeopardy, but his leg was. I don't know how many trips I made to the hospital just to console him. They tried everything they could, and nothing ever made it right. I admired him tremendously because I never got the sense that he was feeling sorry for himself.

I hoped against hope that he could bounce back for his senior year, but it wasn't to be. He just couldn't move. We got him into a game against Kent and he did score a basket.

Among the cards and letters I received after winning the state championship was a hand-written blue note card with a message that was simple and sincere:

Dear Mr. Katte,

I am writing this note to you for all that you've done for me this past year. Your visits in the hospital and your help in class has been very much appreciated. I would especially like to thank you for allowing me to be a part of the basketball team this past season. Upon coming back to school I really wasn't sure if I was going to be accepted back, but you always gave me that extra assurance. You have been more than a coach and teacher. You have also been a friend and for that, I thank you.

Sincerely,

Jim Greenfield

Jim De Groot had the talent to be a Division I player, but he only played one full year for us and he wasn't a great student.

"I didn't care enough about academics. I got through," said De Groot. "Sometimes on game days I would show up late for school. It was just nervousness. My stomach would be going. The next year I think they put in the 'De Groot Rule' that you had to come to school all day if you wanted to play that night. Bob Wilson, the coach at Phillips University in Enid, Okla., showed up at Denver Christian after the season. I visited there,

really liked Bob and signed. Wyoming and Colorado both called after I signed. I asked my dad what I should do and he said, 'You made a commitment.' In hindsight I think I was down the list for CU and Wyoming. I was only a 6'1" skinny kid."

Jim continued to grow and got to be 6'5" by the time he finished college. He had two good years at Phillips, and then went with Coach Wilson when he got the job at Hawaii-Hilo. They went to the national tournament, and Jim made NAIA All-America and is in the school's Athletics Hall of Fame.

With three starters returning from the championship team, we hung at or near the top of the state AA poll for much of the early part of the 1982-'83 season. Kispert stepped into De Groot's scoring role and LeFebre and 6'4" forwards Greg Baltzer and Jay Forseth, whose older brother Eric had been a star on our first undefeated team, provided a potent inside game. Jay didn't quite have the look Eric had on his face but he was very intense also.

With Greg LeFebre (whose son Austin starred for our final team), it's amazing how the apple doesn't fall far from the tree. He never wanted to play outside. He was a blue-collar player who loved to get rebounds and was very tough around the basket.

Kispert was only the second of five Christian players during my 48 years as a head coach to make the varsity as a freshman (the others were Craig Matthies, Toby Schneider, Brian Van Eps, and Alex Terpstra).

He was in Denver Public Schools until he was a freshman, but his mom and dad went to our church and they wanted him at Denver Christian High School. We thought he was kind of soft his first couple of years, but he came on very strong. He was agile and had a nice touch. He could handle the ball, and we used him sometimes as the swingman to reverse the ball on the press. He went on to play college ball at Seattle Pacific University and still holds a business administrative position there.

After Lutheran, behind 31 points from University of Colorado-bound center Brian Cunningham, beat us 62-54 to win the Southern Division title, we lost to Holy Family in the sub-district semifinal, then found ourselves facing three lose-or-go-home games to get to the state tournament.

Having slid to ninth in the state rankings, we bounced back to beat Clear Creek, Eaton (behind 30 points from Kispert) and Brush (Kispert with 30 again) to join our old nemeses Lutheran and Holy Family in the state tournament.

The smart money was on Lutheran, 22-1, ranked first in the state and with the class' most dominating player in Cunningham. The headline in the Rocky Mountain News's 2A preview was: "The line forms behind Lutheran." In prediction pieces that ran before the tournament, we were largely ignored.

We played excellent defense on Gunnison (20-1), holding them scoreless for most of the second quarter and came away with a 65-54 victory. Then we had to come back from 12 points down in the second quarter and hit 13 free throws in the fourth quarter to beat Holy Family 55-52.

We played Lutheran for the fourth time in the season in the finals. We used a diamond-and-one with Forseth responsible for shadowing Cunningham. A balanced offensive performance led by Kispert and LeFebre allowed us to lead from beginning to end, and we claimed a 55-45 victory for our second consecutive title and the fourth in six years.

Chapter 21: How to Score 90 Points and Lose

D uring the retirement banquet a few weeks after my last game, former DC principal Bruce Jansen joked that one day I would write a book, and one of the chapters from a defensive-minded coach would have to be titled, "How to score 90 points and still lose a playoff game."

Well, Bruce, here is your chapter.

One of the things I've always stressed to other coaches, especially young coaches, is that there are going to be nights when absolutely nothing goes your way. We had a good team in 1990. I was confident we had them prepared and that they were ready for the playoffs.

But boy, did it all go wrong.

The saddest thing was that I knew if we had taken care of our business, we wouldn't have been anywhere near Yuma on March 3, 1990. We had won the Metro League championship but slipped up in the district tournament and lost to Kent Denver by a single point the week before.

If we would have won, we'd have hosted a playoff game, and I would have had a two-mile drive to our gym instead of a 147-mile trip to a town of 2,700 people on the eastern plains less than three dozen miles from the Colorado-Nebraska border.

When our bus pulled into town on that Saturday afternoon, we noticed that there was hardly any traffic. As we got closer to the school, we found out why. It seemed like every car and truck in town was parked at the school.

Sports are very important in these small towns, and the whole town comes out to support their teams. They like nothing better than beating a team from Denver. They were certainly ready for us. The only place reserved for our fans was a small roped-off area in the upper right corner of their gym. I think we all could sense it was going to be a long night.

Gary Childress was in his ninth and final year coaching at Yuma High School. His team was undefeated and high-powered. Gary went from Yuma to other coaching positions and then built a powerful program at Grandview High School in Aurora.

Says Gary about that season in Yuma, "We had a great group of seniors who came up through our Saturday morning youth program in Yuma. They were prolific scorers. We had been in the 90s five or six times and scored 116 against Wray.

"Our best players were twin brothers, Bill and Wes Severin, 5-10 guards who were so competitive that if I put them on opposite sides in those Saturday morning sessions, they would often wind up in a fight."

Denver Christian was 18-3, averaging 72 points on offense while giving up just 57 points per game. On paper it appeared to be a classic matchup of a high-powered offense and a defensive-minded team. We opened up in a triangle-and-two zone to try to contain the twins, but Yuma came out pressing and the pace got away from us.

Yuma's 10-point halftime lead swelled to a 104-90 victory for the Indians. Their team would remain undefeated until losing to Berthoud on a late basket by seven-footer Matt Van Abbema, who went on to become the career leader in blocked shots for Western Michigan.

It was pretty ticky-tacky for both teams with fouls called in abundance. We were 26 for 34 from the free throw line. They were 28 for 32. We had four starters foul out, and it ended being the most points a team has ever scored against any team I have ever coached.

Childress has said of that night, "The thing I remember most about that game was that Coach Katte came into our locker room and congratulated us on how well we'd played, wished us luck the rest of the tournament, and said that he couldn't believe his team had scored 90 points and lost."

"I knew about him all through high school—I grew up in Granby and played against Coach Katte's team—and I always said he was the John Wooden of Colorado high school

basketball. Every time he opened his mouth, something good came out. It is incredibly important for young coaches to know how he has impacted this game in Colorado, how Dick just did it the right way for so many years. He is someone I have aspired to emulate."

Chapter 22: Another Tough Opponent — Cancer

One life-threatening medical experience should be enough for any person, but nine years after the aneurysm, I got double-teamed.

I became the president of the National High School Athletic Coaches Association in the summer of 1993. At the national convention in Miami, Florida, I felt the stress of trying to hold board meetings of 53 prominent coaches, every one of them used to being in complete control and wielding absolute power.

That fall while working as side judge for the Colorado State vs. New Mexico football game at Hughes Stadium in Fort Collins, I felt ill and had to leave the field for the first time in my officiating career. I knew something was coming on because I had lost weight and wasn't feeling like myself, but I'm afraid I'm not a very good patient. I refused to slow down and pushed forward with a full plate of teaching, coaching, officiating and my duties with the national association.

My stomach pain got worse, and I thought it could be an ulcer brought on by the stress. Unfortunately, it was a blockage in my small intestine that would require surgery immediately. Dr. Deline removed the blockage and four feet of my small intestine. I was in the recovery room when he told Lorraine and me that the blockage was caused by cancer.

By the time I was transferred to my room, I had no memory of that conversation. My daughter and Lorraine were visiting in the room later and I asked "what did they find in the surgery?" Lorraine had to carefully relay what the doctor had told us in the recovery room, "Cancer." My response to the news was a stony silence. It was hard for me to accept, especially because we were told before the surgery that most often these tumors are benign. I wasn't ready to hear the "C" word.

And there was something else: Cancer had claimed the life of my father.

The doctors believed the surgery had removed all of the cancer, but there was no assurance that it had not spread anywhere else. My belief in preparation and leaving nothing to chance caused me to choose a regimen of chemotherapy.

I felt OK after the surgery but the chemo definitely knocked me for a loop. The treatment started in December, and during the initial week I had daily chemotherapy. It really took its toll. I felt weak, but I never considered giving up coaching. After those first five doses, the routine settled into a 20-minute weekly intravenous treatment for an entire year.

My "scouting report" on the treatment was that if I scheduled the IVs for Monday, it would have the smallest affect on my coaching since most of our games were on Tuesdays and Fridays. Sunday nights were tough mentally, and I felt weak and fatigued after the treatment. However, by Wednesday I was close to normal.

I wanted to take the treatments as privately as possible, so I left school at 7:30 a.m., drove a half-mile to Porter Hospital Cancer Center for the chemo and was back teaching math within an hour. By summer the effects were manageable enough that I often was able to take a treatment in the morning and play a round of golf in the afternoon, and by late summer I felt good enough to begin preparations for another season of officiating football.

The first time I pulled my referee's shirt over my head in Hawaii for the Hawaii-BYU game on September 3, 1994 was a very special moment. I had tears in my eyes because I thought I was never going to be able to officiate again. It felt so good to be back with my crew. Even though I completed my treatments in November and the oncologist was very reassuring, I felt like a lot of cancer patients feel: I might have taken a late-game lead over the disease, but the final score was not yet posted.

Somehow, whenever I have to see my doctor for my physical I think he is going to tell me it has come back. I don't think it ever disappears, it just goes into remission. After 21 years I still say it's in remission.

I was able to take my experience as a cancer survivor and make it part of my final presidential address to the National Coaches Association banquet in Des Moines, Iowa the following spring. I said:

"The Lord gives us these things to be a witness and to use adversity as a testimony. I don't know how I would have made it through without faith. That's what carries you when you really get down. In those weaker moments you can feel the Lord at work in you and experience his faithfulness.

"I think we have a tendency to forget how good God is when things are going well. We think only about ourselves. When you're at the downside of things and things aren't going well is when you really need faith. That's when you can look back and see you've matured as a person and as a Christian.

"We'd had eight or nine years of great teams including one stretch of three years where we lost a total of only three games. I was feeling superior. It's hard for me to say but it may have been God's way of saying, 'You've had success but you're not immune to the things that can afflict any human being.'

"Once I was through the cancer I made a concerted effort to realize how blessed I was. God wasn't through with what He wanted to do with me, and I was determined not to be driven by my own pursuits. I wanted to let Him guide me and take time to smell the roses.

"My setbacks helped me become a better coach because it humbled me. I realized I wasn't in control and that's the hardest thing to learn — especially for coaches. Having the aneurysm and then cancer made that real to me."

"I won't say there weren't moments that I thought, 'Why me?' but my faith has always been that when you look at things in perspective you see God's hand. I used the cancer as a real impetus and grew from that. Hopefully I became a better person, a fuller representative of God's image."

"Adversities are given for a purpose. How you use them is up to you. You can doubt yourself and quit or use them as an experience which improves you as a person and coach, and in your ability to relate to young people."

Following the aneurysm I decided to scale back on how much I was playing with the players. Following the cancer I started using someone else to demonstrate things, and practice became more of a presentation rather than a demonstration. Both of these changes helped me in my coaching. *(Co-author's note: Not completely. At age 75 and two days before his team was to play in the state tournament, Katte wasn't happy about how a player was curling around a screen so he took the court for a spry demonstration of the proper technique.)*

There are a lot of coaches around who play too much because they want to show how good they are but that's not the best way to teach youngsters. I know there are a lot of good coaches who were exceptional players in high school or college but — and this may be a bias from my own playing days — I believe the best coaches are those who might not have been good enough to get off the bench during their playing days or they were role players instead of being stars.

The coaches who didn't have great natural ability are very often the ones who understand how difficult it is for lesser-talented players to master this game and who observed the "big picture" when sitting.

Even though I changed my approach to coaching after the cancer, I remained active as a football official in the Western Athletic Conference and that helped my well-being. It made me keep a good perspective and realize you don't have to be married to basketball year-around. I was able to focus on football from August through November and then step in and be eager for basketball season. My passion for success in coaching basketball was directed more on the lives of the young men I was coaching.

Chapter 23: Teachable Moments from Disappointing Finishes

I have always believed that some of the most valuable lessons to be learned from sports have their roots in defeat.

That said, I won't try to pretend that those lessons are easy to learn or to teach, but they are teachable moments nonetheless. Watching a good team — and a great group of young men — come so close to achieving the ultimate goal but falling short is a painful reminder of the vagaries of the game.

It may be harder to get to a state championship game than to win it, but I have never been able to convince a group of high school players of that as they stood on the court and watched someone else claim that big gold ball on the state championship trophy.

As the century turned to 2000, it closed a decade of Denver Christian basketball during which only three teams did not reach the "Great 8" and two teams suffered three-point losses in the championship game.

We entered the new millennium with a group of players who grew up together, played together and liked to be together. There were two coaches' sons, two with brothers who had played for us, and two unproven sophomores. And on a personal note, my oldest grandson, Rich, was a junior on that team.

They played some memorable games but faltered down the stretch. I think most everyone had expectations that the journey would be longer. But it was more than just the game.

Josh Vriesman described the bus rides as a major bonding point for our teams and life lessons learned: "As I look back at our journeys across the state, I realize that the value of our relationships extended beyond the court. Today, these journeys are a reminder that every moment in life has value. The car rides with our kids, the impromptu lunches with co-workers, the walk around the neighborhood with a spouse ...every moment in our life is an opportunity to share and reflect Christ's love with those we encounter life with,"

The following year brought together a group of players who had only lost one game in the past two years of junior varsity basketball. However, Andy Draayer, the player projected to be our scoring leader, was slowed down by a soccer injury and began the season with his arm in a cast. And it took awhile for the players to establish their roles. We began that season with a verse suggested by Grace, one of our custodians: Zechariah 4:6 " 'Not by might, nor by power, but by my Spirit' says the Lord Almighty."

- Next we established our goals for the season: Play hard, play together and have fun
- Win some we shouldn't and don't lose any we shouldn't
- Be better in February than we were in December
- Win our home games
- Win the Metro League
- Win our district
- Qualify for state
- Win state
- Have great team chemistry and meaningful relationships
- Be a team that represents Denver Christian well and is a positive model of quality basketball

We probably accomplished seven of these 10 goals, and then I gave them these words: "More important than a win is the preparation we make for the win."

The preseason was a struggle—the team lost four in a row for the first time in my career, and parents and players raised some questions. Then two comeback wins propelled us into league play where we went undefeated, and our winning streak reached 18 games as we entered the state tournament.

We travelled to Air Force Academy for the 3A state tournament in 2001. In the opening game we were down by five entering the fourth quarter but pulled away to defeat Platte Valley 63-58. The semifinal game was a classic. Colorado Springs Christian was the top ranked team in the state and had defeated us soundly in December. We were down by two points in the final minute of regulation but forced a turnover. Brian Rooney hit two free throws that would send it into overtime. We fell behind in overtime, but Jason Baker hit a three pointer. Rooney and Andy Draayer converted free throws, and we hung on for a 65-62 victory. The memories of that game have lived in the minds of many people: players, coaches and fans.

Unfortunately, the following night was not quite as exciting. Everyone knew Coach Bob Wood's Buena Vista team was good, but we didn't expect them to come out like they did. His son, Brian, scored 29 points to close out his career as the state's all-time leader in both points and assists and led them to a 71-52 victory. It was frustrating to me that even as a coach that had been on the bench for 827 games, there was nothing I could do to help my team.

Although the final game was a disappointment it can never erase the great team feeling of the night before or diminish the sense of accomplishment of this team and the great senior leadership of point guard Josh Vriesman and Jason Baker (a cross country runner). Both of these players participated in four sports in their junior year because they wanted to contribute as much as they could to the total program of Denver Christian. But they had felt their individual growth was not as great when they spread themselves that thinly so they only participated in three during their senior year.

Each of them spoke openly of the life lessons of basketball. Josh described the memories of that senior year: "This finish didn't include hanging another banner in our historic arena, but it did include a winning streak that carried us all the way into the state tournament at the Air Force Academy. The same Colorado Springs Christian team that dealt us a loss early in the season happened to be in our path in the state semi-finals. We traded blows all game long, eventually going into overtime for the win (I believe they announced that it set a state record for attendance at a high school game during this epic event). The next day we fell to Buena Vista and the state's then all-time scoring leader, Brian Wood.

'The memory of our journey off the court together feels as if it was yesterday. We slowly found our way to the corner tunnel together, turning to watch the Buena Vista squad celebrate the newest addition to their trophy collection. The lessons from my senior season are clearly evident. We could have easily folded up the tents after our 1-4 start, but we didn't. Quitting wasn't an option. Had we quit, we never would have fulfilled our full potential. Another lesson, and one we learned probably more frequently than we would like, but it is through losing we often learn the most. We learn about our resiliency, our courage and our ability to achieve our dreams."

Not only was the team exciting, but that season also marked the birth of "The Blue Crew." Our principal Mark Swalley told the student body to "Cheer not jeer" and have fun. They met that challenge by naming themselves "The Blue Crew." They wore t-shirts with "Blue Crew" which gave the Denver Christian student body an identity. Occasionally they got a bit rowdy and had to be restrained, but being part of the Blue Crew gave the students another reason to come to games, which grew into great fan support.

The Blue Crew has continued until today and expanded to adults and younger fans wearing the Blue Crew t-shirts. The Denver Christian Pep Band was another spirit generating group for many years. They were renowned for the energy they created. Conductors Fred Selby, Tom Ver Straate and others had their groups perform at most home games, and the atmosphere was so up-beat that even I occasionally found myself tapping my foot rather than watching our opponent. They truly inspired our teams!

The loss in the finals in 2001 drove a bunch of hungry juniors to be better the next year. And they were — it was a team that seemed to have it all. Good outside players, size and scoring inside and good chemistry. The young men on the 2001-2002 team began their journey four years earlier, and reached their destination in 2002. More than their ranking of being the best, or the many practices and games, this team's journey was more about the experiences and relationships they shared of being a team that was *Family*. This was a team that played together, shared time in the locker room, sang on the bus and in the shower and just had fun. Winning games certainly added to the team's spirit, but to this group of players, basketball was more than winning or losing.

For Andy Draayer, Brad Jansen and Ryan Velgersdyk that team began more than 10 years earlier—they were elementary school buddies who were inseparable. When they weren't playing ball (basketball, baseball and football), they were together somewhere else. They went to the National Western Stock Show in Denver every year, and loved to be around horses. Each of them had older siblings who were good athletes, so they had been waiting their turn for quite awhile.

As the season began all the members of the team made a pact as they bonded together: "This season we will experience both highs and lows-together we will enjoy the highs and battle through the lows. Remain humble, work hard and most importantly have fun. We have a good year ahead of us. To God be the Glory." This was signed by Andy Draayer, David Fritzler, Ryan Huizingh, Brad Jansen, Ben Kurtz, Daniel Lowrey, Will Norman, Brian Rooney, Evan Sheldon, Bryan Swalley, Tyler Van Eps and Ryan Velgersdyk.

With that commitment unifying them, that group was probably one of the closest teams to ever play the game—always working hard to become the best they could be and enjoying meaningful team relationships. Each individual had the work ethic to become a champion, and their great team chemistry made them champions and fun to watch.

The season began with seven nonleague victories, the closest being an eight-point win at Eaton. Then there was an undefeated journey through the Metro League and a district tournament championship. The regionals were played at Denver Christian and resulted in two convincing wins to send us to the state tournament.

The team was 24-0, ranked first in the state and was a consensus favorite to win the 3A championship. Andy Draayer was Player of the Year in 3A.

The opening game at the Air Force Academy was against the Aspen Skiers with whom we had played some competitive playoff games in the past. This one was no exception, but we broke open a one-point game at the end of three quarters to prevail 51-44 and earn a berth in the semifinals against Cedaredge, from the western slope.

It had been said that the only way our team would lose was they beat themselves, and that's what happened. We hit only 15 of our 55 shots and suffered a 46-40 defeat.

We spent the night wondering what had happened. As hard as we tried, the result never changed. So for a group of young men who always wanted to practice and be together, the season didn't finish as they had hoped. However, the life lessons and memories live forever.

The locker room following the game was quite subdued— almost deathly silent. Even I, a veteran coach, was too stunned to comment. So, I had a prayer with the team, was brief in my comments and asked all of the team members to do some soul searching as we rode back to Denver.

Sometimes the bus ride home was a celebration — this one was very quiet .As we approached home I reminded them that the sun would come up the next morning, and we would again have a chance to play basketball together — for the last time — but for third place.

In Colorado the smaller schools have a consolation bracket as part of the state tournament. And any coach/educator knows that life lessons are more real when dealing with a setback. So we played an exciting consolation game against Platte Valley and lost 62-60 in overtime, ending up in fourth place in the state tournament.

And ten seniors went on to Life after Basketball.

Chapter 24: Another Back-to-Back With a Miraculous Assist

I believe in divine miracles and the power of faith and prayer, but not when it comes to the outcome of games.

It is the responsibility of players and coaches to bring glory to God by hard work, dedication, character and sportsmanship, not the responsibility of God to put His thumb on the scale to affect the final numbers on the scoreboard.

The word "miracle" gets thrown around too much in the sports world, but I have to admit that what I saw from the bench beside the Moby Arena court at Colorado State on the second Friday night in March 2006 at least qualifies as the sports version of Lazarus-like.

We were the defending state champions and brought a 25-1 record into the state semifinal game against Colorado Springs Christian. We had forced a lot of turnovers in our press but the Lions held a 61-54 lead with just 50 seconds to play.

Adding to the dire nature of the situation, our 6'-8" All-State center Brent Schuster had fouled out a minute earlier.

C.S. Christian had made more than 50 percent of their shots and held a 12-board rebounding advantage against us. Even the most optimistic Crusader fan would have to acknowledge that things did not look good.

After they made two free throws to get their lead to seven points I called timeout. My main intent was to keep our players from rushing, to realize the difference between urgency and panic. I told them that time was precious and we needed to force turnovers, but that when we got them we did NOT need to rush and force shots on offense.

One of the best rewards a coach can have is when his team plays with poise under pressure, and to this day I marvel at what our team was able to pull off in that situation.

Point guard Kirk Smith started the rally by penetrating the lane. Jon Adamson slid up the baseline and took a pass from Kirk for a layup that cut our deficit to 61-56. The next 10 seconds were crucial. The Lions broke our press but missed a breakaway layup. If that shot had gone in, I don't think we would have had enough time to come back.

John Lenderink rebounded the miss and we got the ball up court to Tristan Matthies, whose father, Craig, had been the leading scorer on our undefeated team in 1978. Tristan hit a three-pointer from just to the left of the key, and we were within two points at 61-59.

C.S. Christian called timeout, and I told my players that if they couldn't make a steal within 10 seconds, we had to foul whoever had the ball. Honestly, I expected to have to foul, but we didn't need to. In fact, during that entire stretch, we never committed a foul.

Tristan Matthies denied the inbounds pass, Lenderink and Smith trapped the ball and it came loose to Matthies, who backed up behind the three-point line. He'd just made a three-pointer a few seconds before and I expected him to shoot this one. I've always coached my players to make the extra pass and find the open man. A defender was closing hard on Tristan and instead of forcing a tough shot, he passed to Lenderink in the corner.

John was probably the least-likely player on our team to take a shot of this magnitude. He was a sophomore role player with good fundamentals who didn't make mistakes, and he was usually my third man off the bench. But he was playing in crunch time largely because Brent had fouled out. And now here he was with the burden of a state semi-final game on his shoulders.

He hadn't scored a point all night, but he had the confidence to take the shot and hit nothing but net to give us a one-point lead, 62-61.

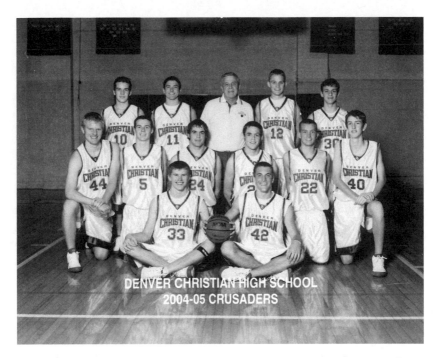

2005 Champions: Back row from left, Brody Matthies, Kirk Smith, Coach Katte, Jacob Vriesman, Tony Ceravolo. Second row from left, Brad Draayer, Blake Zimmerman, Tristan Matthies, Cameron Matthies, J.T. Taylor, Brent Schuster. Front row from left, Dillon Peters, Elliot Van Stelle. (Photo courtesy of Lifetouch National School Studios)

After the game, he told Jon Yunt of *The Denver Post*, "It was a dream come true. I never really pictured myself hitting a big shot like that."

Colorado Springs Christian still had plenty of time to win the game but they missed a runner in the lane and Joe Kurtz, our 6-4 junior who played through injuries most of his career, grabbed the rebound and got fouled.

It was only the Lions' sixth foul of the half and when we inbounded, Cameron Matthies was fouled immediately. He made both free throws to put us up by three, and we kept them from getting off a shot in the final seconds.

The Matthies twins and Schuster were our stars, but we wouldn't have won that game and gone on to the state championship without role players stepping up under pressure.

Up in the stands, Craig Matthies watched, not quite believing what he had just seen. Twenty-six years earlier he had

211

closed his high school career by winning his second state championship and at that time ranked 10th on Colorado's all-time scoring list with 1,746 points.

"All I could think of was, 'The game is over.' It was amazing. I've only seen two or three other games in my life that even came close to that one," said the senior Matthies. "If you could plan out a dream, that would be it."

When I think back about that game or watch it on DVD, it strikes me that I didn't call a timeout, and I'm not sure why. I was either too excited to call it or we didn't have one left. I've always thought that the best thing to do was trust that your players have learned what you taught them and then let them play. If you call a timeout, you also let the other team regroup and maybe draw up something you're not prepared for. I believe in letting them play it out on their own, and this game confirmed that.

I came home that night and told Lorraine that I didn't know how we scored those 10 points. All the details were just a blur.

The championship game wasn't very pretty, but our defense limited Roaring Fork to just 27 percent shooting from the field and Cameron and Tristan combined for 35 points and made seven three-pointers between them. The final score was 68-52 and that was our seventh state championship.

I told Jon Yunt of the *Denver Post* that, "The biblical thing about that is, seven is a number of completeness. I don't know if that means I'm done or...."

The team's comeback was remarkable but I believe they had sown the seeds of their poise down the stretch a year earlier. They had become battle-tested by their experience during the 2004-05 season.

That team had to climb a big mountain to qualify for state. We had talent, but there was much uncertainty when that season began. The Metro League was as strong as ever and the Crusaders were coming off a 16-9 season in which we hadn't finished well. As a result we started the season with a roster that consisted of many new faces.

The most notable loss to the roster was Kirk Nieuwenhuis, a starter in 2004 and a 6-3, 200-pound multi-sport athlete with great talent. He led Denver Christian to our first state football championship as a junior in 2003, running for 268 yards against Eaton during a snow storm in the title game. He was a first team all-state linebacker in 2004. He was a solid basketball player but it was his third-best sport.

Despite his success in football, he was even better in baseball: Metro League Player of the Year as a junior, and the only player from Class 3A to make the All-Colorado team. It was hard for me to argue when he told me he was not going to play basketball so that he could concentrate on baseball. He made all state again, went on to star at Azusa Pacific, was a third-round draft choice of the New York Mets and made his Major League debut in 2012.

We missed his athleticism but Elliott Van Stelle, who had been a reserve the year before, stepped into the role as rebounder and inside presence, the Matthies twins matured as juniors and our senior leadership blossomed. Jacob Vriesman was our point guard who led us by making good choices for us both offensively and defensively.

They were a rewarding group to coach and earned a berth in the Elite 8 in the state tournament at Colorado State University's Moby Gym. What was happening off the court made it a doubly special time in my life.

As the season was heating up in February, I was informed that my alma mater, Calvin College, had chosen me as one of two Distinguished Alumni for 2005.

"Recipients of this award have made significant contributions to their field of endeavor, are recognized by associates for achievements, and manifest a Christian commitment that reflects honor upon Calvin College," the school said in making the announcement.

The honoree has the responsibility to address the alumni, make a presentation to the faculty and speak at Calvin's graduation ceremony. My former student and colleague, Barry Meyer, gave a very flattering introduction prior to my speaking at the Calvin faculty tribute dinner that weekend. Once again I could only say "God is good."

A short time after my selection, it was announced that President George W. Bush would be the commencement speaker

2006 Champions: Back row from left, Blake Zimmerman, Kyle Poland, Brandon Jensen, Brent Schuster, Joe Kurtz, Jon Adamson. Front row from left, Kirk Smith, John Lenderink, Cameron Matthies, Coach Katte, Tristan Matthies, Sean Van Kooten, Brody Matthies. (Photo courtesy of Life Touch National School Studios.)

and that we would be sharing the stage. I was scheduled to speak following his address during the graduation ceremonies at Calvin College that spring. It was a real honor to be on stage with him and to meet him personally.

Around the same time I was selected to the Colorado Sports Hall of Fame. Joining the ranks of such notables as John Elway, Amy Van Dyken, Byron "Whizzer" White, Patrick Roy, David Thompson, Shannon Sharpe, Fisher De Berry, "Babe" Didrickson Zaharias and Jack Dempsey was a very humbling experience.

As fate would have it, the induction ceremony was the same week as the state tournament and every member of our team joined the 800 people in attendance.

The following night we made our journey to Fort Collins to prepare for an 8:45 a.m. game against Buena Vista, coached by Bob Wood, one of Colorado's elite coaches. Bob always got the best out of his players and it's a compliment to say that coaching against him was both a pleasure and a challenge.

Bob won a pair of state championships with the Demons, including a 71-52 victory over us in the 2001 championship game. That game was the high school finale for Bob's son, Brian, who scored 29 points to boost his career total to 2,551, a state record that stood until 2014.

Buena Vista almost got us again in that quarterfinal game in 2005. We led by 21 points at one time, but they got hot in the second half, forced us into two overtimes and had a four point lead with less than two minutes to play in the second overtime. We kept battling, and Jacob Vriesman hit two free throws with 4.4 seconds to play in the second overtime to give us the victory.

One thing we couldn't have known at the time was, if Kirk Neuwenhuis hadn't given up basketball, that game between two Class 3A schools would have featured two players who wound up as starters in major professional sports. We would have had Nieuwenhuis and Buena Vista had Nate Solder, who went on to become an all-America football star at the University of Colorado and then a starter at left tackle for the New England Patriots.

From there, we faced a formidable Pagosa Springs team with Caleb Forrest, who went on to a solid career at Washington State, in the semifinals. Our zone defense took away their inside game and we came away with a convincing 61-49 victory.

In the championship game, Cameron and Tristan Matthies hit some big three-pointers for us early, and we jumped to a 19-4 lead over Roaring Fork. However, they came back with a 19-4 run of their own, and the game was tight throughout the second half. Tristan hit a three-pointer on a pass from Cameron in the last two minutes that finally gave us a little space and we closed it out for a 56-45 victory. I was able to enjoy an experience that had eluded me since 1983: A STATE CHAMPIONSHIP.

I never felt much pressure when we got close so many times. I felt good about my teams and didn't feel like the onus was on my back to prove anything. All of a sudden, the 2004-05 group showed up; they worked hard and overachieved as much as any team I've ever had. As I look back, I believe that year might have been my best coaching job.

One of the two times I thought about retiring was after the '06 team won back-to-back and graduated all those seniors. I thought maybe it was time and I wondered, "Does it get any better than this?'

Throughout my career I've always tried to downplay personal honors. It's not false modesty; I'm proud of what we were able to accomplish at Denver Christian and the way we were able to do it. I believed the recognition we received brought glory to God.

As I reflect back on that time I recall it as a golden time not just for me but for Denver Christian and all the people who had a hand in making that success happen.

One post-script about Bob Wood:

I always knew he had a great sense of humor but I didn't know how good it was until he gave a tribute at the farewell Denver Christian gave for me in April 2012. Bob told the crowd it was ironic he was chosen to speak because he spent so many years coaching a team nicknamed the Demons. He joked that if I was recruiting, I "was going to the same Dutch colony" year after year.

"Many of you probably don't realize that but I'm chasing Dick's record. I only need 22 more seasons of 18 wins a year and I'll have him," Bob said as the crowd broke into laughter. "They all think it's funny, Dick, but you're 75. I'll be 77 then so don't think it can't happen."

Then he turned serious.

"He's humble, credits players and opponents and deflects praise. He's calm. I'm like a volcano ready to erupt and he's like the eye of a storm. He's very competitive. I coached against him in summer league last summer and he's trying to beat me then. He's very respectful. His actions show his heart. He's honest. You ask him something, he'll tell you. He's classy in victory, classy in defeat and he means what he says.

"Basketball mirrors life and he's able to teach life and basketball at the same time. As a coach you have an audience that

The 2006 Champions with their trophy.

wants to listen and it is a great arena in which to be a master teacher. He's a role model. He handles his challenges with grace. He's a coach because he's a leader. To be a leader you have to be a servant. I get a good feeling from that picture in The Denver Post of him sweeping the floor. He's being a servant, getting the floor ready to play so kids who are 18 years old can come out and practice."

I don't know if Coach Wood realized how much his words meant to me that night, but I hope he does now.

Chapter 25: Basketball Through a Crystal Ball — The Game in 2050

When I began coaching at Denver Christian in 1960, John F. Kennedy had just been elected President of the United States. Some young men from Liverpool, England, were trying to settle on a catchier name for their band than "The Quarrymen." What they came up with was The Beatles. By the time I coached my last game, Barack Obama was completing his first term as the nation's first black President.

The amount of change in our culture — and especially its effect on young people — over those years is almost incalculable. A coach who wants to be effective over the long haul must be able to adjust to and relate to the culture of the time.

(Math is a different story. It is like God—it's forever. Teaching methods may change over the years but 2 + 2 will always equal 4.)

I have seen a number of rule changes in basketball during my career. The one-and-one bonus free throw rule after seven fouls in a half has replaced the one-shot free throw. Timeout rules were changed to allow three 60-second timeouts and two 30-second timeouts. The five-second closely-guarded rule was instituted, and the jump ball was replaced (except at the start of the game) with the possession arrow. Most significantly, the three-point shot has had enormous impact on the game at every level. (Some of my players might think I was around when there was a center jump after every basket.)

What does the future hold? Based on some of the evolutionary changes in the game, we might see some of these developments.

- SHOT CLOCK — Time possessions in basketball have been discussed for the past 25 years, probably because of the trickle-down effect from the NBA to colleges to high school. Some coaches believe holding the ball gives them a better chance to win. While that can be an effective strategy, it is not really playing basketball with the objective of putting the ball in the basket.

The National Federation of High Schools has discussed the shot clock almost annually. At the time of this writing, only eight states (seven for boys, one for girls) have adopted a shot clock. I believe there will probably be one in use nationally at some point. My recommendation would be a 40-second shot clock until the last two minutes of the game, and then teams should be allowed to strategize in whatever way suits the situation.

- QUARTERS TO HALVES — I can argue both sides of this debate. For a coach who tries to use most of his roster, a quarter format is probably easier to manage. I like to have at least nine players in the game by the end of the first quarter, but I believe the flow of the game is enhanced when there are no quarters. Going to two 18-minute halves in high school would also eliminate the often-rushed possessions at the end of the first and third quarters.

- THREE-POINT DISTANCE — We may see the line move back a foot or so, but I believe the high school distance is exactly right. It has become a legitimate part of the game and moving it back would make it more of a "launch" than a shot that comes out of the flow of an offense or in transition.

- CHARGE/BLOCK CIRCLE — I am not in favor of this because I think the charge/block is the most difficult call in basketball as it is and this would give officials one more component to worry about. The new NCAA rule says a defensive player cannot move into the path of an offensive player once the offensive player has started his upward motion with the ball. Previously, the defensive player could move until the offensive player left the floor. My opinion could change about the rule depending upon the positioning of the offensive player.

- CLOCK STOPPAGE AFTER A SCORE IN THE LAST TWO MINUTES — I support this. Both the NBA and colleges use it successfully, and I believe it would help to get the ball in play and force action, especially when a team has a lead and chooses not to try to inbound the ball to let the clock run out in the final seconds.

- NUMBER OF TIMEOUTS PER HALF — The last two minutes of the game have become too much "stop and play." Allowing coaches to save all of their timeouts and use them in the last few minutes has created a lot of fan disinterest. It would be better if timeouts were divided into two (one full, one 30-second) for the first half and three (two full, one 30-second) in the second half with NO CARRYOVER. Use them or lose them.

This is my vision and opinion for future changes in high school basketball. I feel good about where the game is today, and I am not trying to think beyond my time, but I can envision several of these things being considered down the road.

Coaches should always dream a little.

Chapter 26:
Leadership

A coach has many faces, and during the course of a game, season or lifetime, most players learn how to read and understand the coach's face. A coach is expected to be a role model, an expert, an enforcer, an encourager, a critic and the LEADER. He must display the qualities of character, composure, commitment, caring enough to confront, communication and creating opportunities. Expectations like this lead to failure. Unfortunately some of the sports community (players, parents, fans) do not have reasonable expectations and are irrational, but I believe it is essential that the coach is rational. In the heat of battle he must remain composed. When dealing with an emotional situation, he must remain calm. Most importantly, I believe if the coach is a good leader he will portray each of these characteristics to some degree.

Leadership is not a quality that can be given. A person can be given authority and be placed in charge. There is a difference between being in charge, being the person with the whistle, and actually being a leader. I can tell in my players' faces if they are following me because I am their leader or because they have to. The old adage says if someone believes in you, they "will run through a wall for you," or that when you say jump, they ask "how high."

Duke coach Mike Krzyzewski says, "In leadership no word is more important than trust. Team leadership will result in team building, earning trust, dealing with adversity and bring out the best in people." The leadership in a coach must be cultivated — most have potential that must "be grown."

The coach as the leader must set the direction for the team. I have always had a long-range plan and a short-term plan, a monthly (seasonal) plan and a daily plan. I try to articulate it both in writing and orally. I do not believe a coach can expect his team to reach their optimum performance if the players do not understand the big picture. They need to know their role — where do they fit in? Why are we doing this? How does everything we do during practice contribute to the final goal of winning games and championships? I have always felt a team would be successful if everyone knew his role and our goals.

When a coach begins his career, he is either going to want the players to "like him" or going to show the players that he "is the boss," I believe every player should know that you appreciate them and that you will help them and be their advocate. I don't advocate "false praise," but everyone who receives instruction or correction will be better if given some praise for contributing to the success of the team, whether it is in practice, during a game or in school. Be sure in all instances, though, to tell the truth. Players deserve the truth, even if they do not want to hear it.

Mike Dunlap who coached two national championships at Denver Metro State University and who also coached in the NBA, had an appropriate phrase about correcting his players: "Praise, prompt, and leave." By that he meant that you can get a player's attention by telling him something he is doing well ("I like the way you are going to the boards"). Afterward, he is more likely to hear your critique, which is why you are talking to him in the first place ("We need you to work harder on help defense – can you do that?"). And then leave it – walk away. Players are more likely to remember the last thing you said to them, and the last thing you said to a player was what he needs to work on (help defense).

The growing of leadership in a coach is a process. I began my career wanting all my players to like me, and that did not work. For whatever reason, some of them will always think they should play more or that you treated them unfairly. I tried to work hard, gain their respect, and to teach them that the most unequal thing I can do is to treat everyone equally. It is important to pay attention to players who don't play a lot. Some of those players probably should not have been kept on the team, but I always wanted a team composed of variety of persons for whom the lessons of life can be gleaned through basketball.

Playing time is one of the major responsibilities of the coach, and I believe you owe it to the entire team to be fair and up front about who plays and who doesn't. Trust in the coach's leadership helps make this tolerable, but every parent wants me to play the four best players and their son. I try to make every player feel as if they have a stake in the overall success of the team. Somehow, I was able to use each of them in practice and most games. Even if they don't play, I always talk to them before they leave. Be aware of jealously or low self-esteem, which can threaten team morale and unity. It will fester if you don't deal with it.

There are many characteristics of good leadership that eventually just happen because the coach is a leader.

- Be the most organized person in your group whether it is in the classroom, gym or in a business. I always had the practice plan tucked in my waistband. Keep your desk orderly so that you always know where things are.

- Don't waste people's time. Have your practices organized down to the minute and follow that schedule. Demand that your players *stand* on the sidelines, waiting to join the action, and make sure they are engaged with what is going on.

- Be positive and optimistic. Convince your players that you have confidence in them. Players can take constructive criticism if they know it is coming from a person who cares about them and believes in them. Sometimes the best attribute a player can have is an allegiance to his coach.

- Admit your weaknesses. It is human to make mistakes, but not too often. Remind them if the team did a certain phase of the game poorly, it probably meant you did not do a good job of teaching it to them. It is good if they know you are willing to examine your actions also.

- Control your temper and hold your tongue. I have tried hard not to lose control and never use profane language or demeaning words towards players. Once you have lost control, you have lost the argument. Remember the toothpaste analogy: once the toothpaste is out of the tube you can't get it back in. Once the words are out of your mouth, you can't get them back.

A leader has to show the face his team needs to see – it will show in his eyes, his walk and his tone of voice. Players today expect their coach to be upbeat, positive and confident they can win. A good leader will present an image that gives that confidence to his team. In a crisis situation I, as the coach and the leader, must embody confidence not confusion, eagerness rather than anxiousness and demonstrate a rational attitude rather than irrational. My face needs to reflect these attributes to my team in a crucial situation. Even when it appears there are no opportunities, my players can trust that their coach is a leader who can create some opportunities for the team.

I firmly believe in the idea that to be a leader, you have to be a servant first. I've always tried to do that. Each one of my players knows that the first thing I do before practice is mop the floor. When I leave, the last thing I do is walk around the locker room and clean up.

Part of coaching is to help young people become leaders, not just better basketball players. From a basketball standpoint, you don't have a really good team if the coach is the only leader.

I've spoken to groups of students who were selected as leaders by their schools. I told them, "You have to realize you're here because somebody sees leadership ability in you. Not everyone has that. It's so hard to define. It's like sportsmanship: You know what it is when you see it, but you can't just give it to someone.

"Leadership is caught, not taught. You have to overcome peer awareness from the social circle. When you see someone sitting alone at the lunch table, go over and sit with him. What you don't realize is that by doing things like that you can create peer awareness to make other students do what you do.

"In high school, some students are going to be recognized because they are athletes, and others are going to emulate what they do. When a popular athlete goes out of this way to greet a young student or someone who isn't a part of their circle, it makes that behavior acceptable to other students."

One of the sad truths I've found is that a lot of males don't want to be leaders. When I was talking to the students on behalf of CHSAA, the ratio was 2-1 girls. I don't know if some boys don't want to take the risk or just don't want to work at it. Some students will use the false humility excuse: "I'm just not good at doing this kind of thing." But someone must recognize that the potential of leadership is there. It is a challenge for each of us as coaches to cultivate and develop the qualities of young players to become men with leadership and character.

Chapter 27: Little Things that Lead to Big Results

W hen I began coaching, summers were pretty much a hands-off period of separation between coaches and players.

The 1970s saw the beginning of fundamentals camps — one or two weeks of concentrated practice on the basics of shooting, passing, dribbling, and defense with coaches. Before long, most high school coaches were running camps for their players and aspiring players.

The '80s saw the camp concept take over basketball and almost all team sports. Most high school teams attended one or two camps each summer, and elite camps and club teams were available for the more advanced players. Soon this spilled over to junior high and middle school, and now much college recruiting is done with 8th and 9th graders at these camps. Many teenagers with big-time aspirations play basketball between seven and eleven months a year now.

In addition to the fundamentals that basic camps teach and the competition which team camps provide, there are *intangible little things* that cannot be measured but determine a player's success. They are the qualities that separate the great from the good and must be emphasized as you play.

As I describe these little things, I will put them into three categories that are distinguished by how coaching can develop them.

The first category contains those on-the-court qualities that players must learn at a young age. It is mandatory that coaches teach these.

    1. SPACING — An important skill that must be mastered both offensively and defensively. On offense, good spacing improves passing angles and gives court bal-

ance. On defense, each player must know how much space to give his opponent to prevent "blow by" (or penetration) and be able to contest each shot. Defensive spacing is different for each player and something each player must learn about his game.

2. FOOTWORK — Being able to jump stop, pivot, square up, get low and stay low, jab, jab and go, drop step, pull up, shoot a "floater, " etc.

3. BE ABLE TO GET OPEN — How to use V-cuts, set up and use screens, possess moves which will free him up and not be predictable in those moves.

4. SHOT SELECTION — Each player must know his area and his spots, should not force shots (either contested or hurried), know about shot fakes and understand "time and score."

5. QUICKNESS AND EXPLOSIVENESS — Physical qualities that each player can improve on with work such as jumping rope, vertical jump, anticipation. The weight room will improve a player's God-given talents and make him a quicker and a better basketball player.

Mastery of these little things will make big things happen for aspiring players.

The second category of intangibles is not made up of physical attributes but the player's nature, the person they are. They are things that only the player has control over, and they make that player a good teammate.

1. ATTITUDE — Attitude more than ability determines a person's success. A positive mental attitude (PMA) can carry a person through many experiences. "The glass is half full, never half empty."

2. TRUST — Believe in one another. Have faith. Always make eye contact. Do nothing behind a person's back.

3. HARD WORKER — Never take short cuts. Have intensity. Go all out always. Play the same whether the coach is watching or not.

4. BE SOMEONE THAT PLAYERS LIKE TO PLAY WITH—Be a good teammate. Let each player choose the other four starters in turn, and it will show which players are good teammates.

5. MENTAL TOUGHNESS — How a person plays when the game is on the line. This is more important than physical toughness. It's how one steps up. Its how a person plays through adversity

These attributes can best be described with our team motto: "Play hard, do your best, be a good teammate and leave the rest to God."

The third category of little things can't be precisely defined, but I know when a person has them.

1. PERSEVERENCE—If things don't work out, do *not* quit. Body language speaks loudly. Don't hang your head and pout

2. HEART—Be someone we can count on.

3. LOYALTY—This character trait has diminished in all walks of life. Have allegiance and attachment. Show respect.

4. CHEMISTRY — Know and accept the role given to you. Understand there is no "I" in "TEAM." **T**ogether **E**very-one **A**ccomplishes **M**ore.

5. COMMUNICATION SKILLS — This is not just a verbal skill. This is hard to teach but a necessity. Young people must learn how to communicate.

Other miscellaneous intangibles include:
1. Listening

2. Not being affected when things are out of one's control

3. The ability to handle adversity

4. Emotional control

5. Being willing to say "I'm sorry"

6. The ability to forgive people (including oneself)

7. Meeting one's potential

These little things are the qualities that every good ball player must possess.

Chapter 28: Milestones — 478, 500, 600, 700, 800, 876

A t some point before the 1990-91 season someone figured out that I was closing in on Bob Chavez' record for the most victories (477) by a boys' basketball coach in Colorado.

Coach Chavez was a legend on the Western Slope. He won three state championships at Glenwood Springs, including an 80-62 victory over us in 1979 that capped an undefeated season for them and cost us a back-to-back.

There were small celebrations at school for my 300th and 400th victories, but when the media got wind that I was approaching the record for victories, we got a lot of coverage.

We had a good team in 1990-91 that defeated schools from the largest classification (Highlands Ranch and Standley Lake) on the way to a 20-2 record. We had a scare against Holy Family, but Cory LeFebre hit a shot at the buzzer to win the game.

The milestone of 478 was reached when we defeated Lutheran 70-57 on Feb. 7. I told Alan Pearce of *The Rocky Mountain News* that I was relieved to have the record behind me: "I'm glad it's over. It's really a relief. My message to all the guys I coach is 'We're a team, and no one person gets the credit.' All of a sudden, though, I'm going against everything I teach and I don't like that."

What I might not have fully appreciated at the time is how much the players and the community enjoyed being a part of those milestone moments. For example, our post player, Tim Veenstra, told Neil Devlin, who covered the game for *The Denver Post*: "I remember being in elementary school and seeing him get 300 and then 400. Now I want to be here when he gets 500."

The record was rewarding, but I would have traded it for a better ending to the season. The only game we lost was to Manitou Springs who had Justin Armour. Armour went on to play both basketball and football at Stanford. We bounced back to win the district title. We defeated Summit to qualify for the state tournament but that's as far as we got. Our team had good size, but we weren't very quick and Salida exploited that in the opening round game. They spread us out, drove past our bigger guys, shot 51 percent to our 39 percent and beat us 64-60. We trailed most of the game, hit three three-pointers to get within two in the last minute. Then we missed a couple of inside shots and couldn't get over the hump at the end.

Dick Connor, the late sports columnist for *The Denver Post*, had a great feel for the preps (his children went to Holy Family). In a column that ran the day the state tournament opened, Dick wrote that Colorado had too many classifications for a state this size and it meant that, with all the teams coming to Denver, some of them were going to play for a state championship at 10:15 a.m. He called me for a comment and I agreed: "That just doesn't seem like a time when championships should be played. I just think you deprive kids of a real glorious moment."

I added my lament at the loss of consolation brackets that had been discontinued, but were re-established when the smaller schools moved to their own venues in Pueblo, Colorado Springs, and Fort Collins.

I know some people are in favor of just packing up and going home after being knocked out of the championship bracket. It's not a lot of fun to play what is regarded as a "meaningless" consolation bracket, but I've never felt that way. I told him, "If we are really in this business for what we say we are, I can do more teaching of young people by having them come back for a consolation game than I can do by winning the whole thing. That's going to sound strange but you have to teach people that life goes on after a loss."

This was also the year that I received the most unusual fan letter of my career.

Jan Boris, a junior high school geography teacher and basketball coach in Czechoslovakia, found my name, and wrote to compliment my style of play and success. I responded to him with some Denver Christian memorabilia and pictures. How he found me back in those pre-Internet days still remains a mystery.

500

Victory number 500 arrived without much media hoopla. One thing I'll always remember about that is that my good friend, Skip Bennett, who coached at Clear Creek, thought that victory number 500 should come on our home court. So he offered to switch that game from his gym to ours. I told him that only a very special friend would do that. It was a very gracious gesture on his part and we did get the victory, but it was only number 499! That is because Eaglecrest nipped us by a point the night before we played Clear Creek. So victory number 500 came a few nights later in a 60-48 victory over Colorado Springs Christian. My children from out of town came to Denver for that milestone and we had a special celebration.

Scott Stocker of *The Rocky Mountain News* reported that I would need 309 more victories to get to the top 10 nationally. But I told him, "I don't think 809 is in the picture."

Again, that milestone year had a bittersweet ending. The 1991-92 team was very solid both offensively and defensively, but we had to survive a last-second missed three-pointer to get past Summit 42-39 in the regional final. At state, we beat Steamboat Springs with 6'7", 250-pound Anthony Barrett (who went on to play four years at Air Force) by 68-59 and then defeated Centauri 56-49 to get back to the championship game.

In the final game we played Hotchkiss. We were bigger but they were quicker, and on the Denver Coliseum's large floor, that can make a difference and it did. They defeated us 81-77 behind Chase Wiening's 30 points. We cut the lead to a point late in the game and they missed a free throw, but got the rebound and put it back in. Bob Tamminga who later played at Northwest Nazarene kept us in it with 34 points, but it wasn't enough.

Afterwards I stood in a hallway at the Coliseum and told Dick Connor, "I feel badly we lost. I don't know of any group of kids that deserved to win more—except Hotchkiss."

600

Temperatures hovered around the single digits on the Saturday night of January 10, 1998 when we played at Sheridan in a typically tough Metro League games. The shooting inside the gym was frigid cold as well. *The Denver Post* reported both teams had more turnovers than baskets, but we were ahead by 10 points after three quarters. Even though we only scored two points (on 1-for-9 shooting) in the fourth quarter, we won the game 43-36 to achieve victory number 600.

With all the media attention, the players seemed more nervous than I did. Our center, Brian Van Epps told Alan Pearce of *The Rocky Mountain News* that "It was real hard. We tried to block it out and treat it like any other game, but in the back of our minds, there was something saying it was for 600." I had a lot of friends and family in the stands, and I told Kevin Coleman of *The Denver Post* before the game, "I hope I don't disappoint anyone."

"I covered one of those milestone games and I asked him, 'Well coach, when are you going to retire?' and he said, "as long as I have something to give and I think that through basketball I can have these teachable moments, I'm going to stay. You can't talk about Denver Christian as a whole, can't talk about Colorado high school basketball, about someone who gave everything he had to mentoring young people, without the name Dick Katte at the top of the list," said Marcia Neville, Emmy Award winning television sportscaster.

At the next home basketball game, the school celebrated the 600th victory. I enjoyed one of the biggest honors of my career when Denver Christian named the gymnasium "The Dick Katte Athletic Center." I was shocked! I felt very honored but also extremely humbled to have this happen while I was still coaching.

With all the attention of number 600 out of the way, we went on to have a terrific year. We were ranked number 1 for most of the season—interestingly the top team in the biggest school class at the same time was defending state champion Columbine, coached by Rudy Martin, whose co-captain, Mike Wolf, is the son of my co-author.

We were balanced, had good depth and played great defense to beat Centauri in the quarterfinals, then defeated top-seeded Buena Vista 62-57 to get to the championship game against Holy Family. We had split with our archrival during the season, but they defeated us 47-44 in the finals.

700

In the pursuit of my 700th victory I was again the beneficiary of another graceful and generous decision by my fellow coaches when Bishop Machebeuf agreed to move their home game to our gym.

Machebeuf coach Paul Bergman told Neil Devlin of The Denver Post, *"It was my decision. It was to show respect for Coach Katte. Dick was trying for his 700th. I was trying for my eighth."*

One of the sweetest things about that 56-35 victory on Jan. 26, 2003, is that we had three sons of former players on the team: Ryan Borger (Bill), Josiah Matthies (Todd) and Jacob Vriesman (Steve).

That milestone was the highlight of the 2002-03 season. Not many of the players on the roster had varsity experience, so when the game was on the line, often we didn't step up. We won games we should have (16) but could not get an upset in any of the others (8).

800

This last "century" milestone of my career had to wait a bit. Although victory number 800 came in a 77-60 victory at Peak-to-Peak on February 19, 2008, it could have come two days earlier against Faith Christian. Faith Christian was ranked second in the state and I'm sure they didn't want to have any part of being on the losing end of a celebration. They defeated us 60-43. *The Rocky Mountain News* reported that I was the

41st coach nationally to achieve 800 victories, and that nine of the coaches were still active.

The team of 2007-08 had great potential and was fun to coach. There were five seniors who were the heart of the team. Beau Baker (6'8"), who received a scholarship to Nebraska-Kearney, and John Lenderink, who signed with Dordt College in Iowa, were the leaders of the team. Even though the season record wasn't impressive (16-8), three of those losses were in "The Tournament of Champions" to big-school teams (Coronado, Mullen and Grandview.) I believed we had the ingredients to be a state tournament team, but we had to travel to Eaton for the regionals, and we finished the season one game short of our goal.

876

Victory number 876 happened in conjunction with our eighth state championship in Pueblo and culminated with an undefeated season. The crowd, the media, and the Denver Christian community celebrated this event and it was a month later before all the hoopla finally settled down.

The second weekend in April was a memorable one for my family and me. The Denver Christian community held a retirement celebration for me that was incredibly special. All of my children and 10 of our 11 grandchildren were there. Our oldest grandson is in the Army and was unable to attend, but his wife and their two children — our first great-grandchildren — joined us. It was wonderful to celebrate those moments with them. Several people gave some wonderful perspectives on my career. My son, Keith, prepared a video tribute with several interviews from coaching friends.

The following evening over 60 of my former players gathered at the Park Hill Golf Course clubhouse for an evening of stories and laughter. Most fulfilling to me was hearing how their experiences on my team had affected the rest of their lives.

Eric Forseth, who was an All-State player on our first undefeated team and is now the provost at Dordt College in Sioux Center, Iowa, wrote a touching letter:

"I wanted to drop you a note to acknowledge the large impact you have had on our family. That Denver Christian was going to be the best learning environment for the Forseths was a decision which we are eternally grateful for and will never regret. As a high school freshman, I came in needing to be redirected. You took the time to redirect me.

"Academically, you managed me in the classroom when I needed structure. It made me a better person and challenged me to grow beyond what I thought possible. This investment yiel0ded a bachelor, master, and doctorate in a few short years.

"Athletically, you cared about how good I could become. You expected the best and everyone knew that you would deal with them fairly and consistently. Our senior year was pure joy. Yes, we won a state championship, but more importantly we made some amazing friends and had amazing life experiences.

"And, you invested in us spiritually. Through these lessons of life you prepared me for the many challenges ahead. You encouraged us often to keep a perspective. You challenged us to keep family a priority. You insisted we take seriously the lessons of Jesus Christ in the Scriptures. You and your wife are to be commended for the many lives you have influenced."

These milestones of numbers, records and honors are behind me, but the milestones in the lives of former players and people in our community are ongoing.

To God Be the Glory.

Chapter 29: Don't Just Retire — Refocus

I've never been a person who has trouble finding things to do, but transitioning from a very structured school and sports environment to retirement presented me with a challenge. How could I step away from a career that had me in the classroom for eight hours a day, then in the gym for two more hours and in the public eye for several months a year?

Like a lot of people, I was fortunate enough to retire in relatively good health. I wanted to cut back on my responsibilities but still be able to find a way to use God's gifts in a way that rewarded me and perhaps inspired others. I wanted to be pleasantly busy rather than stressfully busy.

Over the years, I have been accused of not taking time to stop and smell the roses, but when I finally took the time, I found that they smelled great. You can smell the roses and also find a lot of ways to remain productive.

The opportunities for older Americans to translate the skills that helped them build their careers into meaningful way to help themselves and others have never been greater. Part of the secret, I believe, is your perception of yourself. I don't think of myself as retired; I still think of myself as a teacher, a coach and a leader.

Not long after I retired, I was chosen to coach the Blue team in The Show, an all-star game that mixes players from big and small schools statewide. The Show was played after a Denver Nuggets game at the downtown Pepsi Center. The arena crew had to reconfigure the floor, and we didn't get started until after 10 p.m.

It was a loose game, even by the standards of all-star games. One of my players went to the microphone during a timeout to ask a girl to go to the prom with him, certainly a first in my career. (She said "yes.") The game focused on giving all the players a chance to shine on the big stage.

We fell behind 52-45 at halftime, but I wasn't worried. In the locker room, I told my team not to get discouraged or impatient because the White team had made a lot of three-pointers to score their 52.

"They aren't going to make that many in the second half. You're fine," I told the players.

In retrospect, it was easy to be confident with players like Josh Scott and Josh Adams, who were each just a few months away from being major impact players as college freshmen — Scott at Colorado and Adams (who made a miracle tip-in at the buzzer to win the state 5A championship for Chaparral) at Wyoming — not to mention my own Austin LeFebre, who proved during the game that he could play against stars from the top level of state competition.

I suggested that Josh Scott stay in the low post, where he dominated the second half, and the White team began misfiring from outside. Ahead 86-85 with a minute left, we had the ball and a timeout, but there was no scheme to fall back on. I knew the players had been well coached and that they respected each other's ability.

"Expect a trap," I told them. "I know you don't know each other, but communicate. Talk. Be basketball players."

They handled the pressure very well, and scored the final six points to win the game.

My first summer after retirement was almost as full as usual — but I soon realized that I wouldn't miss spending three days in a college dorm at team camp.

A few weeks later, I coached my last "official" game at the Coaches All-Star game in Alamosa. Austin LeFebre hadn't made a three-pointer all season, but he hit one at the buzzer to tie the game. We dominated the overtime to give us a victory. It was nice to have one last Denver Christian victory moment.

My contacts in the game and with CHSAA have kept me active. I live only a few blocks from the University of Denver, and the Pioneers' coach Joe Scott invited me to come over as an unofficial observer to watch practices and share my observations. In addition, CHSAA tapped me to be an eyes-and-ears coach representative at games across the state. Together, Lorraine and I enjoyed spending evenings at many different gyms observing the game-night atmosphere.

I didn't expect to return to the bench on a regular basis, but then I heard from Bill Hanzlik, former NBA player and coach and now the executive director of the Gold Crown Foundation, which sponsors a full array of youth sports and enrichment programs in Denver. Bill talked me into coaching a team in Gold Crown's High School Development League for students who had either been cut from their school teams or just wanted to play organized basketball. The league had tripled in size from the first year, and the players just loved the game and wanted to have fun.

I signed on for this task because I'm still a coach at heart, and coaches coach. I've always believed that if you are able to contribute something to the development of young people then you have a responsibility to do so. And in the back of my mind, I thought that maybe I could help at least one player make his high school team the next year.

"I knew Dick was extra special when he wanted to help coach after retiring in our Gold Crown Foundation prep development league development League. His presence helped convince over 150 kids from 35 different high schools to play in our league and develop their game. His commitment to these kids who thought they couldn't ever play again has truly changed many of their lives," said Bill Hanzlik, ,CEO of the Gold Crown Foundation, a 10-year NBA player, former head coach of the Denver Nuggets and a member of the Colorado Sports Hall of Fame

I assumed it would be pretty casual, but when I was on the bench and my team was going up and down the floor in front of me, all my old instincts come right back. The games weren't official, and the results were not going to be in the paper the next morning, but it was still important to these players and their families.

I found myself saying the same things to these players that I had during 52 years of high school coaching.

"Nice move, Justin."

"Great pass, Adam."

"C'mon, you're better than that."

"Don't stand. Always do something after you pass the ball."

If I had a quarter for every time I've said those things, I'd need a boxcar to store them.

Many of these players were oriented both academically and athletically. It wasn't unusual to see the players sitting along the gym walls doing homework between games.

The league had garnered an impressive coaching staff. I enjoyed the camaraderie of my fellow coaches, all of whom were very accomplished. Dave Lawrence won both boys' and girls' big-school state championships at Horizon. Scott Smith enjoyed a reputation for getting the most out of his players during a successful career at nearby Alameda High School where the basketball court is named for him. Former NBA first-round draft choice Mark Randall of Cherry Creek High School played on an NCAA runner-up at Kansas. Stu Howard was head coach at Englewood for 29 years. Bill Garnett, a star at Regis High School and Wyoming, was the fourth player chosen in the 1982 NBA draft. Rudy Martin, who coached a state championship at Columbine and whose teams were perennial state contenders, now coached the girls' team at Green Mountain. Duane Lewis, the acclaimed Shot Doctor, occasionally dropped by to share his expertise on shooting selection, form, and technique.

I didn't treat these players much differently than I did the ones I coached at Denver Christian. I tried to stay positive, recognizing the level of skills they had, but I also admonished and corrected—because if these players were to get better, they had to hear the bitter with the sweet. I wanted them to be coachable.

The Gold Crown experience was enjoyable, but my biggest contribution to the game and the culture of high school sports was getting the chance to appear at seminars and symposiums around the state to talk to coaches, athletes and most importantly athletes' parents.

One of these events was the Southwest Colorado Sports Symposium in Durango. *Durango Herald* reporter Jim Sojurner, who was not long removed from being a record-setting pole vaulter for Pine Creek High School, did a concise job of summing up the key message from athletes to parents: "Show up, and shut up."

My message to parents was blunt. Far too many parents care more about their own child's line in the box score than they do about the success of the team. They have come to see sports as a way to pursue college scholarship money and, sometimes, as a means to bragging rights about their child.

I offered one piece of advice that might have surprised some parents—let your child fail. I have taught young men to work hard; some things are beyond their control. That's a lesson parents need to learn too.

I know the symposiums were well received, and I will continue to work as an ambassador in a joint effort with CHSAA and the Positive Coaching Alliance.

Some students just don't get math — they have math anxiety. Since I never lost my love for math, even in retirement, I found myself volunteering to sit beside those who struggle and giving them some positive success in their math courses. Once

Katte tutoring Denver Christian students in math, which he does twice a week. From the left, Hayden Langerak, Junior Cisneros, Robert Nino and Daija Jenkins.

a teacher, always a teacher. Now, I help a handful of students at Denver Christian, where I work in a math lab for a couple hours twice a week. It is good to see their progress; they look forward to the days when I come.

My retirement almost seemed providential for my church, where I have always been very active. A few months after I retired, our pastor took a call to a new church and that presented a need for leadership. I was able to give much time and energy because in retirement, there is no schedule.

However, I am very careful to hold onto what I call "my time." Some twenty years ago, when I was still working and actively officiating, I ran regularly to stay in shape. I chose to do that immediately after waking up at 4:30 a.m., so I wouldn't procrastinate — a forty-five minute daily workout. At that time of day, there were no distractions or interruptions. It became my time to meditate and think about things. When I retired from officiating, I didn't want lose that special time — nor did I want to keep running — so I began a two-mile daily walk.

Now, since retirement, I no longer get up at 4:30 a.m., but I do find a time each day for my walk. I walk alone, and it's my time to think and pray as I walk — just me and my God. I strongly recommend to everyone, especially coaches, a daily quiet time. Amidst the stress and busyness of the coaching life, a quiet time is very beneficial.

Yes, indeed, I was able to refocus and receive fulfillment in a variety of activities. I was blessed in my career, and now am trying to give back — to be a blessing in the lives of people searching for success and to give back to a game that gave me so much.

Chapter 30:
Random Thoughts After 52 Years in the Game

I
n this final chapter, I have listed some thoughts that are an important part of my view of the game. Some of these are also included in other places in this book. Many of these thoughts can be applied to all aspects of life. I don't know who originally said many of these, but I do know that I have repeated them all.

- "Attitude more than Aptitude determines your Altitude." — *Motivational speaker Zig Ziglar* (What you become is determined more by your attitude than your talent.)

- Good coaching is best defined as developing character, attitude and values as you teach fundamentals and team play.

- "Discipline is knowing what to do, when to do it, and doing the best you can every single time." — Bob Knight (Too often discipline is viewed as punishment.)

- Coaches must DEMAND and DISCIPLINE without being DEGRADING. (We don't improve by being belittled.)

- The greatest mission of a coach is to teach about LIFE AFTER BASKETBALL (not to teach "Basketball is Life"). What will the lessons of basketball do for you after 5, 25, 50 years?

- Be a focused BENCH COACH – you must have the ability to alter the outcome of the game once the game has begun (alter the game's momentum: control tempo, use time-outs, substitutions, offense and defense adjustments, etc.).

- Two of the most important aspects of basketball, which are very hard to teach, are REBOUNDING and MENTAL TOUGHNESS. There is no home-court advantage in rebounding and defense. They are caught, not taught — it's about HEART.

- Sometimes a player's greatest challenge is accepting his role on the team. (Each of us must know our place...)

- Don't be affected or spend time on things you cannot control (officials, surroundings, facilities, opponents).

- Coaches have a tremendous opportunity, but also an awesome responsibility. You will be amazed what your players take from you. Be a good role model and mentor (for the game and for life).

- The most important thing in a person's life is his faith (trust) and that will result into good team loyalty and chemistry.

- "Be quick, but don't hurry" — *John Wooden* (Don't play out of control.)

- There are very few things in life we do better when we are angry – players must realize this and coaches must keep their emotions under control. ("...Slow to become angry..." — *James 1:19.*)

- "The whole is greater than the sum of its parts" should describe your team. (This is not true in mathematics, but it is true in basketball.)

- "A life is not important except in the impact it has on other lives." — *Jackie Robinson's tombstone*

- An offensive player should not get himself in the air (with no place to go).

- Be sure you know what's happening when you are talking – insist on eye contact and undivided attention from the players.

- Understand Time and Score – at the end of the clock, be sure your shot selection doesn't give your opponent the ball with time to score.

- "You have to strike a match to start a fire, you have to turn a key to unlock a door, you have to care and love to open a heart" — *Jimmy Bryan, coach of four state championship teams at Glass High School in Lynchburg, Virginia and former mayor of that town*

- Players must do more than LISTEN, they must HEAR and DO (especially in timeouts — they must be reminded of what you have told them).

- "You can never work too much on shooting." — *Morgan Wooten*

- You get what you tolerate and what you expect – young people live up to our expectations.

- "It is the point guard's job to get the ball across half-court and start the offense – it doesn't start with the point guard shooting." — *Guy Gibbs*

- "Two in a Row" has many applications in basketball (turnovers, missed free throws, stops, shots, etc.). Coaches just create an awareness of this.

- It is good to have your basketball season described as a journey – and to remember that the "journey is the destination."

- "The greatest joy one can have is doing something for someone else without any thought of getting something in return." — *John Wooden*

- Players must understand floor spacing (15-17 ft.) and balance (spread the floor).

- Be sure to play all of the players you will want in the game sometime in the first half (8 or 9 players).

- Parents will always want you to play "the 4 best players" and their son.

- There are "DEFENSIVE NO-NO 's" — no lay-ups, no second shots, no uncontested shots and no fouls.

- The "F-word" in basketball is FINISH — how you finish is what counts. (We all know people that do everything right, but do not deliver...)

- Make your opponents drive right or left, but don't allow the penetrating drive.

- Make your opponents do what they don't want to do (i.e., make them play your game).

- The warm-up before the second half is more important than the pre-game warm-up — the first five possessions of the second half often determine the pulse of what is to follow.

- Open gyms without having a coach present are just wasted time — players work at their own pace and learn bad habits.

- "Create good people and the rest will follow." — *Walt Whitman*

- It is wise to give players a two-minute rest sometime in the first 12 minutes — they will then "have their legs" down the stretch.

- A coach is wise to insist on "no discussion" with disgruntled parents within the first 18 hours following the game. This results in a more rational conversation and better results.

- Get the shot we want rather than the quick shot that your opponent gives – don't FORCE your shots.

- "We don't do conditioning drills because everything we have done in practice has given us conditioning." — *Russ McKinistry, winner of 418 games and two state championships in 25 years of coaching in Colorado, now head coach at Castle View*

- "Be kind and gracious to your students, let them really know you care about them. There is no doubt that a high school coach can make the greatest impact on a student." — *Jimmy Bryan*

Let me finish with these thoughts that are NOT random. They are the heart of my philosophy.

1. Work hard, do your best, be a good teammate, and leave the rest to God. This is how we challenged our teams to play in the past years and it is an excellent focus in basketball and for all of life. As John Wooden described in his PYRAMID of SUCCESS: "Success is the peace of mind which is a direct result of self satisfaction in knowing you did your BEST to become the BEST that you are capable of becoming."

2. Good sportsmanship is a goal for every team I have coached, so I will describe what that means to me. Sportsmanship is an attitude, and attitudes are caught, not taught. It is a value that young people are developing. Values are established in the home, and modeled and nurtured in school and in competition.

   - "Sportsmanship is: winning with class, losing in style, always being positive and going the extra mile."— *from the Kansas State High School Activities Association*

   - Sportsmanship is like beauty – it is hard to define, but you know what it is when you see it. Sportsmanship is the impression, that the public receives and leaves the game with. The score is soon forgotten, but the conduct and attitude remains forever in the minds of those who were most affected.

   - Respect, integrity, fair play and courtesy are components of citizenship that are probably taught best through sports. With these values the spirit of competition thrives, fueled by good rivalry and graceful acceptance of the results. It is how you control yourself, whether things are going for you or against you and how you react to adverse conditions.

- Sportsmanship is a journey and we certainly have NOT reached our destination but we are headed in the right direction. This journey into life should permeate our character and lives.

3. "Be more concerned with your character than with your reputation, because your character is what you really are, while your reputation is merely what others think you are." — *John Wooden*. Our coaching has been successful if our players become men of character.

The qualities that we expect of the young men who are products of our program are good values, the ability to make good choices and good character. Probably the finest of these qualities that a player can attain is Christian character. If nothing more is accomplished by our basketball program than the development of such character, it has been successful. It is a quality that is hard to measure, but it is always tested.

The success that Denver Christian enjoyed can never be misinterpreted as the purpose (philosophy) of the program. The banner hanging in the center of the gym says, "To God be the Glory." That spirit and belief of Christianity must always permeate our play, individually and as a team, both in winning and in losing. By our play and our example, these words must be our Christian identity.

Chapter 31: Honors and Records, By the Numbers

The plaque is not large, but for what it means to me, it could be a billboard. Dave Sanders, a business teacher and the girls' basketball coach at Columbine High School, was shot and killed on April 20, 1999 while shepherding students to safety amid a murderous rampage that claimed not only Dave's life but those of 12 children.

In his memory, the *Denver Post*, along with coach Sanders' family, inaugurated The Dave Sanders Colorado Coach Award to be presented annually to a high school teacher and coach. The first award was given posthumously to Dave. I remain humbled and honored that the second award, in 2000, was given to me.

The words on the plaque that hangs directly in my line of vision when I sit at my desk read "In honor of his commitment, most notably in the area of girls' athletics, this annual award is presented to a high school coach and teacher who has not only achieved longevity and success in their field but who also has demonstrated outstanding character while doing so."

I didn't know Dave, but we had a mutual friend. Al Harden, former head basketball coach at the University of Denver, coached Dave at Fountain Central High School in Veedersburg, Indiana, and they stayed in touch over the years. The floor in Fountain Central's gymnasium is now the "Dave Sanders Court."

Being inducted into the Colorado Sports Hall of Fame in 2005 was the biggest sports-related honor of my career but nothing eclipses being mentioned in the same company as Dave Sanders, a teacher who made the ultimate sacrifice by putting himself in harm's way to protect students.

Other awards and honors in no chronological or prestigious order:

- MAX Preps National Coach of the Year 2012
- Denver Post Coach of the Year all-classifications 2012
- National Federation High School Hall of Fame, 2004
- National High School Basketball Coach of the Year, 1996, 2008
- Colorado High School Coaches Association (CHSCA) Hall of Fame, 2000
- National High School Coaches Association Athletic Director of the Year, 1995
- Colorado High School Activities Association Hall of Fame, 1999
- Colorado All-Century High School Coach, 2000.
- Metro League Hall of Fame, 1986
- Calvin College Distinguished Alumni Award, 2005
- Dwight T. Keith Award for Outstanding Service to National High School Athletics, 2000
- Don DesCombes Award for exceptional leadership and service to the Colorado High School Coaches Association, 1991
- Numerous "Coach of the Year" honors by *The Denver Post*, *Rocky Mountain News*, *Colorado Sidelines*, and Metro League.
- Inaugural winner of the CHSCA Dick Katte Sportsmanship Award, 2013
- CHSCA Tom Sutak Award for contributions and achievements in high school basketball, 1983
- CHSCA Teacher-Coach Award, 1988

Dick Katte's presence in the Colorado High School Activities Association Record Book.

All-time victories

1. Dick Katte, Denver Christian, 876-233, (1964-12)

Victories at 1 school

1. Dick Katte, Denver Christian, 876, (1964-12)

State Championships

1. Rudy Carey, Denver East/Manual 9
   (1988,90,91,96,99,2004,07,08, 14)

1. Ron Vlasin, Merino/ Littleton 9

3. Dick Katte, Denver Christian, 8,
   (1970,78,80,82,83,05,06,12)

Championships at 1 school

1. Dick Katte, Denver Christian 8,
   (1970,78,80,82,83,05,06,12)

Consecutive State Championships

1. Ron Vlasin, Merino, 5, (1976-80)

2. Ken Niven, Alamosa, 4, (1989-92)

3. Ken Shaw, Regis Jesuit, 3 (2009, 10, 11)

4. Dick Katte, Denver Christian, 2, (1982, 83)

4. Dick Katte, Denver Christian, 2, (2005, 06)

4. Jim Smithburg, Flagler, 2, (1981-82)

4. Steve Hill, Ridgway, 2, (1994-95)

4. Merlyn Henry, Bennett, 2, (1986-87)

State Tournament Appearances

1. Dick Katte, Denver Christian, 25, (1970-73, 76, 78-83,
   88, 91-92, 94-95, 97, 98-99, 01-02, 05-06, 11, 12)

League Championships

1. Dick Katte, Denver Christian, 23, (1970, 72-73, 76-84,
   90-94, 97, 98, 01, 02, 11, 12)